The Impact
of Structural Adjustment
on the Population of Africa

The Impact
of Structural Adjustment
on the Population of Africa

The implications for
Education, Health & Employment

Edited by
Aderanti Adepoju

UNFPA
in association with

Heinemann
PORTSMOUTH (N.H.)

James Currey
LONDON

United Nations Population Fund (UNFPA)

in association with

James Currey Ltd
54b Thornhill Square
Islington, London N1 1BE

Heinemann;
A Division of Reed Publishing (USA) Inc
361 Hanover Street
New Hampshire 03801

*A study prepared within the framework of the project
'Population, Human Resources and Development in Africa'
with the financial support of UNFPA*

British Library Cataloguing in Publication Data

Impact of Structural Adjustment on the
Population of Africa: Implications for
Education, Health and Employment
 I. Adepoju, Aderanti
 338.96

ISBN 0-85255-405-2 Paper (James Currey)
ISBN 0-85255-406-0 Cloth (James Currey)

Library of Congress Cataloging-in-Publication Data

The Impact of structural adjustment on the population of Africa : the
  implications for education, health & employment / edited by
  Aderanti Adepoju
      p.   cm.
   Includes bibliographical references.
   ISBN 0-435-08085-7 (Heinemann)
   1. Africa, Sub-Saharan--Economic conditions.   2. Africa, Sub
   -Saharan--Social conditions.   I. Adepoju, Aderanti.
   HC800.I48   1993
   330.967--dc20   93-20329
                                                               CIP

Typeset in Adobe Garamond, 10½/12 pt, by Opus 43, Cumbria, UK
Printed in Great Britain by Villiers Publications, London N6

Contents

Notes on
Contributors

Aderanti Adepoju, an economist demographer, was formerly professor at the Universities of Ife and Lagos in Nigeria and currently the United Nations Population Fund (UNFPA) Training Coordinator for the Project Population, Human Resources and Development in Africa at the African Institute for Economic Development and Planning, Dakar, Senegal.

C. Chipeta is a professor at Chancellor College, University of Malawi, Zomba, Malawi.

Josie W. Eliott is the Head of the Department of Economics at Fourah Bay College, University of Sierra Leone, Freetown, Sierra Leone.

Theophilus Oyeyemi Fadayomi was, until recently, a research demographer and director, Social Development Department, Nigerian Institute of Social and Economic Research, Ibadan, Nigeria. He is currently a senior demographer in the African Development Bank, Abidjan, Côte d'Ivoire.

Tayo Fashoyin is Professor of Industrial Relations and Personnel Management, Faculty of Business Administration, University of Lagos, Nigeria.

Jane Wanjiku Kabubo is a tutorial fellow at the Department of Economics, University of Nairobi, Kenya.

Karamoko Kane is the assistant dean, Faculty of Economic Sciences, Cheikh Anta Diop University and an associate at the African Institute for Economic Development and Planning, Dakar.

Mafuku Kintambu is an economist at the University of Kinshasa, Zaire.

Mumpasi Lututala is a demographer in the Department of Demography, University of Kinshasa, Zaire.

Matingu Mvudi lectures at the Department of Economics, University of Kinshasa, Zaire.

I. Mwanawina is at the Department of Economics, University of Zambia, Lusaka.

Francis Mwega is a senior lecturer in the Department of Economics, University of Nairobi, Kenya.

Wilred A. Ndongko was director of research in the Institute of Human Sciences, Yaoundé, Cameroon. Currently, he is a senior regional adviser at the Economic Commission for Africa, Addis Ababa.

Deji Popoola served as head, Department of Industrial Relations and Personnel Management, University of Lagos. Currently, he is regional adviser, International Labour Organization, Nairobi, Kenya.

Nii Kwaku Sowa was formerly head, Department of Economics, University of Ghana, Legon, Ghana. He specializes in economic policy analysis, money, banking and finance.

This book is dedicated
to the increasing number of Africa's poor,
who today have less access
to health, education and employment opportunities
as social expenditure has drastically declined

Acknowledgements

Aderanti Adepoju

This volume emanates from collaborative research activities between the editor and a network of African researchers in several African universities. These researchers have ingeniously drawn from a variety of scattered data sets, often fragmentary and incomplete, to focus attention on the rapidly deteriorating conditions of living in the region, in large part as a result of the structural adjustment measures. Needless to state, the views expressed by the authors do not necessarily reflect those of the organization for which the editor is currently engaged.

Several colleagues, too numerous to name, provided useful comments on the drafts of the reports prepared by our collaborators. However, the following persons deserve particular mention: Dr P.O. Sonaike, Messrs Fred Murphy and Ernest Harsch for their editorial assistance, advice and comments.

The publication of the volume is made possible through the project Population, Human Resources and Development in Africa, funded by United Nations Population Fund (UNFPA). The volume would also be used as a training manual for the project's trainees and widely disseminated to similar training programmes.

The project secretaries worked tirelessly through the series of drafts. Everyone associated with the volume would no doubt be delighted to see it eventually published and used by trainees, researchers, policy makers and the donor community involved in promoting the well-being of Africa's population.

Preface

Lamine Ndiaye
Director, Africa Division
UNFPA, New York

Several African countries have made important sacrifices to implement the economic recovery programmes and adjustment measures and have encountered immense social and economic problems especially huge increases in unemployment (compounded by lay-off of workers in both private and public sectors), reduction in real wages and drastic reduction in resource allocation to the critical social sectors, especially education and health.

It is often argued, for instance, that structural adjustment programmes sometimes are 'incomplete, mechanical and of too short a time perspective'. In the process, human resource development (and utilization) has received very low priority in structural adjustment programmes and consequently, education and health have been particularly hard-hit. This situation could further retard efforts for long-term development and exacerbate inequality and poverty. The call for adequate resources for the implementation of structural adjustment programmes with human concerns at the centre is therefore most appropriate, with adequate attention also to population dynamics, its causes and consequences.

With continued cuts in government spending in several African countries, per capita spending on health and education plummeted in absolute terms. Subsidies on health care, food, education, etc. have frequently been the first targets of austerity budgets. All these have resulted in stagnation, and increasingly in reversal in some key social sectors.

In most African countries, the vulnerable group have been affected both by the impact of recession and decelerated growth and crucially by the consequences of adjustment. Indeed, it is widely accepted that in Africa, people today are poorer than they were at the beginning of the 1980s.

It is in the light of these and other considerations that the current research project focuses on the socio-economic implication of the structural adjustment programme (SAP) on the population of Africa. The selected country case studies include those that have implemented, and a few countries which are currently in the process of initiating, reform policies. In all cases, attention is focused on three key sectors – education, health and employment, with emphasis on consequences for human resource development *and* utilization. After all, human resources are Africa's main asset.

Abbreviations

AAF-SAP	African Alternative Framework to Structural Adjustment Programmes for Socio-Economic Recovery and Transformation	MINEDUC	Ministère de l'Education Nationale
		NAP	New Agriculture Policy
		NCDP	National Commission for Development Planning
ACP-EC	African-Caribbean-Pacific-European Community	NDE	National Directorate of Employment
		NGOs	Non-Governmental Organizations
AIDS	Acquired Immuno Deficiency Syndrome	NLC	Nigeria Labour Congress
		OECD	Organization for Economic Cooperation and Development
BAD	Banque Africaine de Développement		
BEAC	Banque des Etats de l'Afrique Centrale	OCA	Agency for Agricultural Marketing
CBN	Central Bank of Nigeria	PAM	Minimum Agricultural Programme
CFA	Communauté Financière Africaine	PASS	Adjustment Programme for Social Sectors
CHC	Community Health Centres		
CHP	Community Health Posts	PAMSCAD	Programme of Action to Mitigate the Social Costs of Adjustment
COCOBOD	Ghana Cocoa Marketing Board		
CRAD	Regional Centres of Development Assistance	PFP	Policy Framework Paper
		PHC	Primary Health Care
CSO	Central Statistical Office	PIP	Public Investment Programme
EdSAC	Education Sector Adjustment Credit	PNDC	Provisional National Defence Council
ERP	Economic Recovery Programme		
EPI	Extended Programme of Immunization	SAP	Structural Adjustment Programmes
		SDA	Social Dimensions of Adjustment Project
FNE	National Employment Fund		
GDP	Gross Domestic Product	SDR	Special Drawing Rights
GLSS	Ghana Living Standards Survey	SFEM	Second-Tier Foreign Exchange Market
GNP	Gross National Product		
HIV	Human Syndrome Immuno-Deficiency Virus	STD	Sexually Transmitted Diseases
		TBAs	Traditional Birth Attendants
IDEP	African Institute for Economic Development and Planning	UEPA	Union pour l'Etude de la Population Africaine
IFIs	International Financial Institutions	UIESP	Union Internationale pour l'Etude Scientifique de la Population
ILO/JASPA	International Labour Organization, Jobs and Skills Programme for Africa		
		UNDP	United Nations Development Programme
IMF	International Monetary Fund		
INDECO	Industrial Development Corporation	UN-ECA	United Nations Economic Commission for Africa
INS	Institut National de la Statistique		
IRES	Institut de Recherches Economiques et Sociales	UNESCO	United Nations Educational, Scientific, Cultural Organization
LDCs	Less Developed Countries	UNICEF	United Nations Children Fund
MAN	Manufacturers Association of Nigeria	UNFPA	United Nations Population Fund
MCHP	Maternal and Child Health Posts	UNIP	United National Independence Party
MDC	Malawi Development Corporation	VAT	Value-Added-Tax
MESIRES	Ministère de l'Enseignement Supérieur et de la Recherche Scientifique	WHO	World Health Organization

Introduction

A. Adepoju

African economies have experienced numerous disruptions since independence in the 1960s. In virtually all African countries, the steady growth of the early years after independence gave way to stagnation and eventual decline. Among Africans, the optimism that greeted political independence has now been replaced by widespread despondency. Whilst other parts of the world have prospered significantly, the region has become impoverished in absolute and relative terms. The whole of sub-Saharan Africa is now facing the need for some form of economic restructuring.

At independence, most African economies were geared towards primary commodity production (mostly agricultural), which accounted for the largest share of the gross domestic product (GDP). For example, primary production contributed 48 per cent of GDP in Zambia over 1964–9, 39 per cent in Kenya in 1964–8, and 64 per cent in Nigeria in 1960. Manufacturing sectors, based mainly on import substitution, were very small absolutely and relative to other sectors, contributing only 2 per cent of GDP in Ghana in 1957, for example. Each country's exports were dominated by just a few commodities: cocoa in Ghana, Nigeria and Cameroon, copper in Zambia and coffee and tea in Kenya. These accounted for up to 75 per cent of export earnings.

During the first decade of independence, many economies were open and the government sector was small indeed. However, countries such as Ghana and Zambia soon embarked upon programmes of state control to the extent that the share of government consumption in GDP in Ghana increased from 10 per cent in 1957 to 18 per cent by 1989. Government involvement in economic activities eventually developed into bottlenecks to development, as many public sector enterprises, riddled with inefficiency and corruption, consumed more and more scarce resources.

Nevertheless, many economies grew at significant rates: real GDP grew by 6.5 per cent a year in Kenya in 1964–73, 15 per cent in 1964–9 in Zambia, and 5 per cent in Sierra Leone up to 1972. Despite high population growth rates of around 3 per cent a year, per capita income also increased significantly, by an annual average of 13 per cent in Zambia in 1964–9, 3.4 per cent in Kenya in 1964–73, 2.2 per cent in Ghana in the 1960s, and 2.5 per cent in 1964–79 in Malawi. At the same time, inflation was moderate in many of these countries: in Malawi it was 6.5 per cent per annum between

1965 and 1975, and in Kenya it averaged 3.4 per cent between 1964 and 1973.

However, in the late 1970s and early 1980s most African economies went into slump. Zambia's GDP stagnated between 1970 and 1985, whilst population increased annually at 3 per cent. Real growth in Kenya averaged 4 per cent between 1974 and 1990, down from 6.5 per cent. In Sierra Leone it dropped from 2 per cent a year in 1975–80 to zero in 1983–7. The decline was registered in virtually all economic sectors. In Ghana, for example, food production in 1983 was only 72 per cent of the 1971 level. Exports fell in both volume and value, bringing foreign exchange constraints, whilst imports rose, bringing balance-of-payments problems. During the same period, Malawi's exports declined by 40 per cent while imports increased, resulting in a deterioration in the net barter terms of trade of 30 per cent and an increase in the current account deficit from 7 per cent of GDP to 18 per cent in 1980. In many countries, foreign reserves fell below the normal expectations for international trade. Inflation soared as a result of inadequate domestic production and lack of foreign exchange for imports. Kenya's inflation rate increased from 3.4 per cent annually in the pre-1974 period to 11 per cent in 1974–90. In Malawi it rose from 6.5 per cent in 1965–75 to 10 per cent in 1975–84, and persistently thereafter.

Throughout the period, government spending consistently outstripped revenues, resulting in large domestic bank borrowing at the expense of the private sector. For example, domestic bank borrowing in Sierra Leone increased by 330 per cent between 1980 and 1985. In Malawi, the overall budget deficit rose from 6.2 per cent of GDP in 1977–8 to 11 per cent in 1980–1. Foreign borrowing also increased to meet budget deficits, worsening debt service obligations in foreign exchange.

In the case studies in this book, the factors identified as responsible for economic deterioration include adverse weather conditions, such as drought in Cameroon (1982–3), Kenya (1974–5, 1979–80, 1983–4), and Ghana (1978–9, 1982–3); the oil crises of 1973–4 and 1979–80, and the resulting world economic recession and collapse of the international oil market in 1981 (affecting Nigeria specifically). Above all, increased protectionism by developed countries, relatively high external interest rates, decline in the inflow of concessionary capital, and the deterioration in the terms of trade worsened the already poor economic situation. Other contributory factors were price controls, physical import restrictions, direct government involvement in economic activities, imprudent borrowing in the late 1970s, maintenance of over-valued currencies, mismanagement and corruption, and political instability.

Stop-gap efforts were made to try to address the deterioration, including currency devaluation (Sierra Leone devalued three times between 1983 and 1986), exchange controls, import restrictions, 'austerity measures' and even government declarations of a 'state of emergency', all to no avail. Low growth, poor export performance, high debt burdens, and severe financial imbalances finally forced many African countries on to the road of economic reform. They agreed that the problems were fundamental, requiring restructuring not short-term palliatives. Since the late 1970s and early 1980s in particular, about 30 countries have adopted structural adjustment programmes (SAPs) with the approval and financial support of the World Bank and IMF, while a few others have pursued reform independently of the Washington-based institutions. Senegal adopted an initial structural adjustment programme with the IMF in 1979 to cover the 1980–3 period, but implementation was interrupted in its first year. Another agreement was then negotiated for 1986–9. Although Ghana formally adopted a World Bank and IMF supported SAP in 1986, it had earlier launched an Economic Recovery Programme in 1983 which, in both content and orientation, was a forerunner of the SAP. Kenya attracted its first structural adjustment loans from the World Bank in 1980. By 1986 most African countries had embarked on structural or financial recovery programmes, with or without the help of the IMF and World Bank.

The IMF/World Bank inspired SAPs are based on an orthodox approach, with aims broadly similar in all the countries: they give greater weight to growth objectives than to income distribution objectives. This 'growth first' strategy is reminiscent of the neoclassical growth models of the 1950s and 1960s. Consequently the principal objective is to realign overall domestic expenditure and production patterns in order to bring the economies back to a path of steady and balanced growth.

The policy measures attached as conditions to formal stabilization and structural adjustment loans aimed at overcoming short-term imbalances. This involved contractionary measures to achieve short-term stabilization and restore equilibrium in the balance-of-payments through expenditure-switching measures designed to reduce the level of aggregate demand. Often this meant reducing budgetary deficits, relating prices to market levels, liberalizing trade, adjusting exchange rates (mainly through devaluation), and controlling the supply of money and credit. In most cases specific targets and time limits were set for major macroeconomic indicators.

These programmes aimed at institutional reform, including public enterprises and parastatals. They gave preference to private sector enterprises over those in the public sector and used market-determined prices to influence production and consumption patterns. They likewise favoured export promotion, reinforcing the orientation of African economies toward uncertain external markets. In essence, the programmes assumed that the economic crises afflicting African economies flowed from domestic policy shortcomings. If external factors were taken into account at all, they were seen as largely conjunctural.

From the beginning, structural adjustment has been highly controversial across the African continent. Although many Africans acknowledged the need for sweeping economic reform, they were not convinced that the prescriptions put forward by the Bretton Woods institutions necessarily provided the best remedy. Some criticized the programmes for their narrow emphasis on fiscal and monetary mechanisms, others for paying little heed to long-term development objectives.

There is consensus among the authors of this volume that, in the countries surveyed, one does not find a strong association between adjustment policies and economic performance. There are strong indications that adjustment policies may not be able to guarantee that African countries will overcome the effects of external shocks even in the long run, unless there is a more favourable external environment.

In many African countries pursuing structural adjustment, what progress there has been has been confined to nominal growth in GDP, without any transformation of the structure of the economy. Ghana, for example, achieved an average annual growth rate of 5 per cent over 1984-8. But manufacturing capacity utilization has remained low, at 35 per cent in 1988. In Nigeria it was just 38 per cent in 1986-7. In most countries covered in this volume, small and medium enterprises have been marginalized by the exchange rate and trade liberalization measures. High domestic interest rates, resulting from restrictive monetary and credit policies, created disruptive business climates. Industrial closures were rampant. Four out of ten banks were shut down in Cameroon, whilst in many countries marketing boards for major commodities were scrapped.

Although agriculture grew modestly in these countries, production of food stuffs declined. In Ghana, production of cereal fell by 7 per cent and starchy staples by 39 per cent between 1984 and 1988. Other countries had similar experiences. Although export earnings generally increased, imports also rose, intensifying the balance-of-payments crisis. Some countries recorded budget surpluses because of curtailment of public expenditure and improved revenue collection through taxation and cost recovery measures, which had harsh effects on the citizens. Prices continue to rise.

In some countries, institutional and political constraints, high social costs and inadequate financing made it difficult to sustain reform. The direct impact of the measures has created disillusionment and resistance to further restructuring, especially in the face of stagnation or decline in per capita consumption. For example, in 1986 Zambians found the conditionalities too harsh and the government broke with the IMF agreement. Subsequently the IMF and the World Bank stopped funds to Zambia, which had to adopt a go-it-alone recovery programme. In Sierra Leone it became obvious that structural adjustment had failed, due to overly ambitious objectives, administrative weaknesses, and unbearable social costs. The programme was abandoned in 1988, after the country's president had declared a state of economic emergency.

Among the many criticisms of structural adjustment, the most common refrain has been that it has tended to ignore the human element. When austerity hit, it was the 'soft' social sectors – education and health above all – that often saw their budgetary allocations cut most drastically. In addition, because of higher prices and reductions in public sector employment levels, people's living standards declined, especially in the urban centres. UNICEF, the United Nations Economic Commission for Africa (ECA), International Labour Organization, and many others have drawn attention to a serious erosion in social services, wages, and employment levels associated with structural adjustment, and have pointed out that it has been the most vulnerable sectors of society – the poor, women, children, and the aged – who have suffered the most (Cornia, 1987; Onimode, 1989).

A UN-organized conference concluded that 'Adjustment measures have been implemented at high human costs and sacrifices' and are 'rending the fabric of African society' (Khartoum, 1988). Former UN Secretary-General Javier Pérez de Cuéllar found that 'The most vulnerable population groups . . . have been severely and adversely affected, directly and indirectly, by such measures as the withdrawal of subsidies on staple food items, the imposition of limits on wage increases . . . the retrenchment of civil servants and private sector personnel frequently belonging to the lowest salary categories, and the cutting of expenditures on social services, including health and education, and on basic infrastructure.' (UN, 1988).

Taking into account some of the perceived shortcomings in 'orthodox' SAPs, the ECA in 1989 issued the 'African Alternative Framework to Structural Adjustment Programmes for Socio-Economic Recovery and Transformation', which placed adjustment within a longer-term developmental perspective emphasizing human resource development and the maintenance and improvement of social sectors (ECA, 1989). Later that year the World Bank itself acknowledged some SAP shortcomings. The move away from the earlier 'basic needs' approach was 'a mistake; every effort should be made to protect basic needs expenditures in times of recession' (World Bank, 1989). The Bank recognized that the poorer and more vulnerable sectors of the population could be hurt by some short-term adjustment policies, and that special measures were necessary to protect them and the social sectors more generally. In Ghana, Senegal, and elsewhere, the Bank and other donors began to support special programmes to 'alleviate' the negative impact of adjustment measures on the most vulnerable sectors of society.

Since then, the discussion has moved beyond 'tag-on' poverty-alleviation measures to standard SAPs. It has recently begun to encompass the concept that the human element must be central to the entire development process, indeed, that 'human development' must be its ultimate purpose (UNDP, 1990). Therefore, if short-term economic reforms and adjustment measures become necessary, they should from the outset be designed in such a way that those elements that contribute to human development – education, health care, living standards – are not unduly jeopardized.

In line with such concerns about the impact of economic reform *on the people of Africa*, this volume seeks to examine the available empirical evidence on the socio-economic implications of structural adjustment programmes on the continent. It endeavours to do so through a series of detailed case studies of ten African countries, selected from the different geographical regions of sub-Saharan Africa and representing a varying range of adjustment programmes. For each country, the studies seek not only to give a broad overview of the adjustment process, but also to systematically assess the impact of such programmes in three key areas: education, health, and employment.

The authors of these studies have faced numerous difficulties, some methodological, some empirical. How does one distinguish between the impact of structural adjustment programmes and that of broader economic difficulties? Would the social sectors have fared better or worse without the adjustment programmes? One solution adopted by many of the authors has been to compare budgetary expenditure on education and health with other areas of government spending to shed light on any shifts in priority during SAP periods. Such conceptual dilemmas have been compounded by data that is often incomplete and unreliable – a problem frequently encountered in Africa.

Whatever gaps there may be in the data, however, the general trend is apparent – deterioration in the social sectors. The health situation improved only slightly in a few cases and in some others has worsened. In Ghana, life expectancy at birth increased from 44.8 years in 1960 to 54 years in 1987 due to improved health facilities. But the patient/physician ratio increased from 13,740:1 in 1965 to 14,890:1 in 1984, as emigration of skilled personnel intensified, while population grew appreciably. The hospital fees introduced as a result of the SAP cost recovery strategy resulted in declines in hospital attendance. Spending on health declined in most countries. In Zambia, it fell at an average annual rate of 18 per cent. Health expenditure as a percentage of the budget also declined. In Nigeria, budgetary allocations for health fell short of the 5 per cent of national budget advocated by the World Health Organization (WHO). In 1990, per capita allocation to health was a mere US$0.62!

Education has also been hard hit by SAP. Its share of total spending declined in most countries. Inadequate facilities brought overcrowding and pupil/teacher ratios reaching as high as 63:1 (100:1 in some areas) in Cameroon and Malawi. The primary school population enrolled in Ghana fell from 69 to 63 per cent between 1965 and 1986. It was 47 per cent in Malawi in 1988–9 and is 40 per cent in Sierra Leone. In Nigeria it fell from 90 to 64 per cent in 1980–7. The transition rate from primary to secondary school has also dropped (from 67 to 47 per cent in Nigeria between 1979 and 1984). In Sierra Leone, the estimated illiteracy rate is as high as 85 per cent and may reach 98 per cent in rural areas. Cost sharing schemes were introduced in all the countries, while some have withdrawn subsidies on student meals and books at boarding schools. Faced with declining resources, some parents have withdrawn children from schools.

The studies also reveal that structural adjustment resulted in shifts in the labour market, marked declines in industrial job opportunities, and rising unemployment, particularly among graduates. In Cameroon, formal sector employment grew at an average of 3.7 per cent over 1977–86, compared with 8.3 per cent in 1968–77. Similarly in Malawi, the rate dropped from 8.3 per cent in 1967–77 to 3.7 per cent in 1977–86. Unemployment rates have increased in almost all the countries covered because of contractionary fiscal and monetary policies which resulted in retrenchment of workers. Urban unemployment rates rose to 14.8 per cent in Sierra Leone, over 60 per cent in Zambia between 1985 and 1990, and from 10 per cent in 1986 to more than 12.2 per cent in 1987 in Nigeria. Only in Ghana did unemployment as a percentage of the labour force drop, from 2.8 per cent in 1984 to 1.9 per cent in 1987.

In most countries, despite economic improvements in a few areas, there has been a decline in the extent and quality of education and health care, and formal sector employment has fallen, sometimes drastically. Much of the blame rests with the economic crises that preceded structural adjustment, but clearly the adjustment measures themselves contributed significantly to this decline. Now that the importance of protecting social sectors and living standards is more widely recognized, one might hope that economic reform in Africa will be designed to ease human suffering, not contribute to it.

References

Cornia, Giovanni, Richard Jolly, and Francis Stewart (eds) (1987). *Adjustment with a Human Face, Vol. 1: Protecting the Vulnerable and Promoting Growth.* Oxford: Oxford University Press.

Cornia, Giovanni, Richard Jolly, and Francis Stewart (eds) (1988). *Adjustment with a Human Face, Vol. II: Ten Country Case Studies.* Oxford: Oxford University Press.

Economic Commission for Africa (1989). *African Alternative Framework to Structural Adjustment Programmes for Socio-Economic Recovery and Transformation.* E/ECA/CM.15/6. Addis Ababa.

International Labour Office (1992). *Report VI: Adjustment and Human Resources Development: International Labour Conference 19th Session 1992.* Geneva.

'Khartoum Declaration: Towards a Human-Focused Approach to Socio-Economic Recovery and Development in Africa', declaration of the International Conference on the Human Dimension of Africa's Economic Recovery and Development, Khartoum, Sudan, March 5–8, 1988. Addis Ababa: United Nations Economic Commission for Africa.

Onimode, Bade (ed.) (1989). *The IMF, the World Bank, and the African Debt, Vol. 2: The Social and Political Impact.* London: Zed Books.

Palmer, Ingrid (1991) *Gender and Population in the Adjustment of African Economies: Planning for Change (Women, Work and Development N.19).* Geneva: International Labour Office.

United Nations (1988). 'Mid-term Review of the Implementation of the United Nations Programme for African Economic Recovery and Development 1986–1990: Report of the Secretary-General'. A/43/500. New York.

United Nations Development Programme (1990). *Human Development Report 1990.* New York.

World Bank (1989). *Sub-Saharan Africa: From Crisis to Sustainable Growth.* Washington.

2 Ghana

Nii Kwaku Sowa

The 1980s was a time of severe economic depression for most developing countries, and above all for sub-Saharan Africa. Ghana was among those where the decline was so drastic, even cataclysmic, that it made international headlines.

At independence, Ghana's per capita income stood at a comparable level to that of Mexico or South Korea, and it was classified as a medium-income country. Growth slowed in the following two decades, with Gross Domestic Product (GDP) per capita increasing at a rate of only 2.2 per cent per annum in the 1960s and declining by 0.5 per cent per annum in the 1970s. By the beginning of the 1980s, Ghana's economy was in crisis.

In April 1983, the Provisional National Defence Council (PNDC), under Flt Lt Jerry Rawlings, accepted an International Monetary Fund (IMF) programme for economic recovery and structural adjustment. The measures aimed principally at eliminating market distortions that prevented price mechanisms from allocating resources efficiently. They also sought to reorganize the productive structure through price incentives. The latter benefited mainly the tradable sector of the economy. A range of monetary, fiscal, incomes, and exchange-rate policies were utilized to achieve the objectives.

Since then, Ghana's economic recovery has been hailed as a world showpiece, mainly owing to the country's macro-level performance during the initial years of the programme. While GDP had been persistently declining in the pre-adjustment years, it began showing positive growth rates once again. By 1985, inflation had dropped to 10.9 per cent from its 1983 rate of 123 per cent. These signs of recovery made Ghana one of the most credit-worthy nations in sub-Saharan Africa. By 1988, Ghana had received all six of the credit facilities programmed by the IMF.

These gains at the macro level, however, did not trickle down to the micro level. Indeed, some of the policies implemented brought hardship to certain vulnerable groups in the economy.

This chapter examines the socio-economic impact of the structural adjustment programme in Ghana. We look first at the macro-economic background, examining the structure of the economy, its decline, and the consequences of that decline. Next, the

7

adjustment measures proposed and implemented are discussed, and the effects of adjustment on various sectors are analysed. Conclusions and recommendations are offered in the last section.

Macro-economic Background

While Ghana's economic structure has always been heavily weighted toward the primary sector, the latter has gradually been yielding some of its share to the tertiary sector. Expansion in government services was especially marked under the Nkrumah government (1957–66), which, declaring socialism to be its goal, increased state participation in almost every sphere of the economy. Between 1957 and 1969, the share of government consumption in GDP increased from 10 per cent to 18 per cent, while private consumption declined from 80 per cent to 70 per cent. Manufacturing also took off during those years, increasing from 2 per cent to 9 per cent of GDP and growing to 10 per cent per annum, owing to the high priority the Nkrumah government placed on import-substitution industrialization. Still, the secondary sector as a whole maintained the same relative share of GDP, reflecting a relative decline in mining and other secondary industries.

Cocoa continued to dominate exports, but was not growing. There was no clear policy to develop agriculture to supply the newly established industries, which instead relied on imported raw materials. Hence the attempt to make the country self-reliant through import substitution made it dependent upon foreign exchange. Low productivity persisted in agriculture: while this sector was the largest employer, it contributed proportionately the least to GDP. The neglect of cocoa without an appropriate substitute contributed immensely to the decline of Ghana's economy.

Subsequent governments after Nkrumah and the National Liberation Council that succeeded him (1966–69) did little to alter the structure of the economy. By 1982, agriculture's share of output had increased to 51 per cent, but the nation was still not producing enough to feed itself. Indeed, the mounting proportionate share for agriculture was due mainly to a decline in manufacturing (from 15 per cent in 1969 to 8 per cent in 1982). Faced with severe foreign exchange constraints, the country could no longer import the necessary inputs for industry, and capacity utilization fell to less than 25 per cent.

The 1970s saw the country's output declining while population increased at a faster rate (Table 2.1). Exports dropped in both volume and value, with cocoa falling below the levels of the late 1950s. As the foreign exchange constraint tightened, shortages arose in imports of both intermediate and consumer goods. By the early 1980s, inflation was running at three digits, the balance of payments was very unfavourable, cocoa and other export revenues were at their lowest point, and unemployment and underemployment were high. All in all, a classic case of stagflation, with shortages of almost every conceivable item: food, raw materials, even water. The country's plight attracted international attention when in 1983 – amid drought and bushfires – nearly a million Ghanaians were repatriated from Nigeria.

This decline can be attributed to both internal and external factors. Unfavourable terms of trade and unfavourable weather conditions, especially the drought of the late

1970s and early 1980s, were among the causes. Ghana's economy is fragile, too dependent on a few primary exports, especially cocoa and timber. Unstable commodity prices on the international market make these unreliable sources of earnings. Even as the Nkrumah government was creating industries and providing social and economic infrastructure, the international price of cocoa was in continuous decline. Like other oil-importing countries, Ghana also suffered from the oil crisis and the global slump of the 1970s.

Table 2.1. Ghana, basic indicators of economic performance, 1960–88

| | Average annual growth rates | | |
	1969–70	1970–82	1986–8
Gross domestic product	2.2	–0.5	5.4
Gross domestic investment	–3.1	–5.1	16.9
Exports	0.1	–4.7	4.7
Imports	–1.5	–4.8	10.5
Terms of trade	1.1	0.2	–
Total agriculture (volume)	2.6	–0.2	1.9
Food production	2.6	–0.2	–
Population	2.3	3.0	–
Labour force	1.6	2.3	–

Source: World Bank, Toward Sustained Development in Sub-Saharan Africa (Statistics Annex), Washington, 1984; GSS, Quarterly Digest of Statistics, Accra, March 1989.

Despite the declining terms of trade, the country maintained a rigid, fixed exchange rate and refused to devalue. As goods became scarce, the government resorted to price controls, introducing further distortions and bringing in its wake unprecedented levels of corruption. Kalabule, a system wherein the 'haves' took advantage of scarcities and exploited the 'have-nots,' became the order of the day and reached its height in the early 1980s.

Gross mismanagement, corruption, and political instability also contributed greatly to the economy's decline. Policies simply remained on paper or failed to be implemented because of coups d'état or other changes of government. Ghana has had at least four development plans drawn up since independence, but none have been implemented fully. Monetary and fiscal policies were either not geared to the realities of the situation or not properly applied. For example, little was done to broaden the tax base during the time the nation was engaged in opulent spending. Expenditures have been on the increase ever since independence, while state revenues have continually dwindled.

We can summarize the internal causes of economic decline as follows:

1 maintenance of a fixed and highly overvalued exchange rate that discouraged exports and produced huge profits for traders of imported goods;
2 large budget deficits, financed mostly by printing money, which resulted in inflationary pressures and further distortions of effective exchange rates;

3 imposition of price controls at the manufacturing stage, which discouraged production and offered excess profits to the unregulated small-scale trading sector; and

4 misallocation and misuse of import licences, leading to further inefficiency and denial of critical inputs and equipment to high-priority areas.

External factors included:

1 adverse weather conditions in 1978–9 and 1982–3, seriously reducing agricultural output;

2 sharp increases in petroleum prices in 1979, followed by world recession;

3 deterioration in the terms of trade, and especially the continual decline in the world price of cocoa;

4 the expulsion of more than a million Ghanaians from Nigeria in 1983.

Consequences of the Crisis

The most general consequence of Ghana's economic decline has been the general impoverishment of the nation as a whole. Per capita GDP, at constant 1975 prices, dropped from 634 Cedis (₵) in 1974 to ₵395 in 1983. Most people by then could not afford such basic necessities as food and shelter. The near-famine situation caused many people to have 'Rawlings' chain,' a slang term for the protruding clavicles caused by hunger. *Kalabule* became the order of the day. Food production per capita fell to about 72 per cent of the 1971 level. While health standards had improved markedly in the preceding two decades, there was a severe deterioration in the early 1980s. Life expectancy at birth had increased from 46 years in 1970 to about 55 years in 1979, but now fell to 53 years. Daily calorie intake as percentage of requirement fell from 88 per cent in 1979 to 68 per cent in 1983.

The crisis also sharply affected personnel development and labour. High inflation rates were not matched by increases in the nominal wage, and real incomes eroded. Many took on second and third jobs, the most common of which was trading. 'Trading' need not be in actual wares – some made huge gains simply by knowing someone in a position to give them ration chits for 'essential commodities'; these were in turn sold for cash to the actual traders. Such recourses hardly encouraged personnel development, as drop-outs were better off becoming 'businessmen' than staying in school. Skilled personnel such as doctors, engineers, and teachers who could not engage in *kalabule* took flight to other African countries or to Asia. By the beginning of the 1980s Ghanaians of every class and skill were leaving in droves for Nigeria, which in turn led to their expulsion in 1983 after declining oil revenues brought on economic crisis in that country.

The Recovery Programme, 1983–8

Ghana's acceptance of the IMF/World Bank–sponsored Economic Recovery Programme (ERP) in 1983 came as a surprise to most analysts, in as much as the Provisional National Defence Council (PNDC) was widely perceived as anti-capitalist.

But the decision is understandable in the light of the pressure of the desperate economic situation.

The initial programme aimed at stabilizing the economy and arresting its decline; a second phase, begun in 1986, was more concerned with restructuring to foster growth and development. The discussion which follows makes no distinction between the two phases. The stated objectives were:

1   to restore incentives for production of food, industrial raw materials and export commodities, thereby increasing output to modest but realistic levels;
2   to increase the availability of essential consumer goods and improve the distribution system;
3   to increase the overall availability of foreign exchange in the country, improve its allocation mechanism and channel it into the selected high priority activities;
4   to lower the rate of inflation by pursuing prudent fiscal, monetary and trade policies;
5   to rehabilitate the physical infrastructure of the country in support of directly productive activities; and
6   to undertake systematic analyses and studies leading towards a major restructuring of economic institutions in the country. (Republic of Ghana, 1984–6: 15–16)

In pursuit of these goals, a range of fiscal, monetary, and regulatory policies have been adopted.

Exchange rate adjustments

A system of multiple exchange rates first replaced the long-standing practice of fixing the Cedi at 2.75 to the US dollar. Later, the Cedi was again fixed, first at 30 and then, after a series of devaluations, at 90 to the dollar. A two-window system was next introduced, with official transactions pegged at 90 and all others at a rate determined through weekly auctions. By June 1990 the Cedi had depreciated to 327=US$1 at this Window 2 rate. 'Forex bureaus', introduced in 1988, are privately owned foreign-exchange dealerships that determine their own sale and purchase prices. The bureau rate stood at around 340=US$1 at the end of 1989. The overall depreciation of the Cedi through these various mechanisms has implied the loss of an implicit tax on foreign-exchange transactions. Without accompanying fiscal changes, this could have meant monetization of a higher deficit and further inflationary pressures.

Fiscal management

Since the introduction of the ERP, government spending has been strongly curtailed. Cost-saving and cost-recovery measures have been introduced across a wide range of departments and services, including redeployment and retrenchment of thousands of public employees, introduction of hospital fees, and removal of subsidies to education (see below). Concomitant efforts to increase revenue collection and widen the tax net have combined with the spending cuts to produce the elimination of recurrent deficits after 1986. Surpluses since then have been running at about 0.5 per cent of GDP.

Divestiture

After independence, the state had taken on the role of entrepreneur, but most of its enterprises proved to be liabilities rather than assets. Under the adjustment programme, the government has sought to sell off some state enterprises and put others up for joint-ventureship. These include the state fishing corporation, certain hotels, and some industries run by the Ghana Industrial Holding Corporation. But the private sector, hampered by lack of financing and management expertise, has not been prepared to step into the breach. Uncertainties as to the supply of inputs and the marketing of finished goods also tend to drive those with the resources into commerce rather than manufacturing. A task force has been established to develop incentives to private investment, but no coherent policy in this regard has yet been forthcoming. The Investment Code of 1985 provides more incentives to foreign than to local entrepreneurs.

Trade liberalization

Most restrictions that impeded the effective functioning of the market have been removed. Price controls on most commodities have been eliminated, and even interest rates are allowed to fluctuate free of Bank of Ghana intervention. Restrictions on international transactions have also been eased: Ghanaians travelling abroad may take out up to US$3000; exporters may keep retention accounts abroad in which a certain percentage of their export earnings may be kept.

Manufacturers have objected to difficulties they face under trade liberalization, but government maintains that it cannot provide protection for inefficient industries indefinitely. Still, a revised tax structure adopted in 1988 does provide some protection to some industries. Four levels of duties ranging from zero through 35 per cent are applied to goods categorized as exempt, concessionary, standard, and luxury respectively. In addition, the 1988 budget provided for protection to selected drugs, garments, cosmetics, mineral waters, juice, rubber sandals, soaps, and certain food products. With the special taxes, it is estimated that protection of between 25 per cent and 90 per cent has been offered to some industries.

The Economy Responds

The recovery and adjustment programmes seem to have salvaged Ghana's economy from a near-bankrupt situation. GDP growth resumed, after registering negatively during the preceding decade. Indeed, a record 8.96 per cent increase in GDP was recorded in 1984, and for the entire 1984-8 period average annual growth was 5 per cent. All sectors had positive growth rates, with utilities and manufacturing producing the most striking results (Table 2.2).

These successes can be credited to the recovery programme, if not to its policies *per se* then at least to the inflow of external funds that fulfilment of the plan's conditionalities made possible. Renewed availability of foreign exchange made it possible to rehabilitate some manufacturing concerns and provided raw materials for inputs. Capacity utilization is now roughly estimated at 35 per cent. However, given industry's small share in the economy and the low base from which it is growing, it will still be some years before industrial growth will have a major impact. Nor have all manufacturing firms gained from adjustment: medium- and small-scale enterprises in

Table 2.2. Ghana, percentage change in GDP by type of economic activity, at 1975 prices

Activity	1981	1982	1983	1984	1985	1986	1987	1988
Agriculture	-2.56	-3.25	19.11	9.71	0.65	3.31	0.04	3.58
Industry	14.46	16.67	-6.77	11.94	17.60	7.56	11.34	10.27
Mining and quarrying	-7.34	-8.38	-13.64	13.49	6.45	-3.03	7.89	35.82
Manufacturing	-19.27	-20.49	-11.17	12.90	24.32	10.95	10.01	9.24
Electric and water	11.86	-8.11	-38.91	42.96	20.73	18.03	18.73	6.74
Construction	-4.79	-91.15	27.43	2.33	2.81	-2.66	15.02	4.55
Services	2.73	4.65	4.54	6.63	7.52	6.50	9.38	7.83
Wholesale and retail trade, hotels and restaurants	-1.92	-10.38	-5.26	10.15	13.68	9.02	17.45	7.41
Transport, storage and communication	6.76	1.30	7.26	12.76	8.45	5.62	10.89	10.18
Finance, insurance, real estate and business service	1.66	-1.38	14.12	9.26	2.58	7.66	5.48	6.73
Community, social and personal services	15.23	-4.99	7.09	20.10	7.76	46.02	19.20	5.98

Source: Calculated from data obtained from IMF, Financial Statistics and GSS, Quarterly Digest of Statistics, Accra, March 1989.

particular have been marginalized by the exchange-rate and trade-liberalization measures.

The service sector, which already had an uncomfortably high share of GDP for a developing country, also maintained a robust growth rate, with commerce the fastest growing subsector. This was no doubt facilitated by trade liberalization and the new exchange rate policies.

In contrast, agriculture has grown only quite modestly, raising questions as to the long-term sustainability of the adjustment programme. Agriculture is the backbone of the Ghanaian economy, contributing about half of national output. Yet with the exception of 1984 – a year of particularly good rains – most years have witnessed low growth rates. Cocoa production did pick up, increasing from 166,700 tons in 1984 to 288,800 tons in 1988. Local producer prices increased while the world price continued to fall, a consequence of the devaluation of the Cedi. Such devaluation also made it less attractive to smuggle cocoa to neighbouring countries, causing the volume exported from Ghana to increase.

But the benefits to the cocoa sector failed to spill over to other agricultural producers, for whom the altered terms of trade did not operate as favourably. The relative prices of foodstuffs to cocoa declined steadily in 1983–7 (Table 2.3). Production declined as well; cereals, from 1.07 million tons in 1984 to 995,000 tons in 1988, and starchy staples, from 11.17 million tons in 1984 to 6.82 million tons in 1988. It is worrisome that the country is neglecting the production of the very commodities on which its survival depends.

Table 2.3. Ghana, relative prices of food, 1977–87 (1977 = 100)

	1977	1980	1981	1982	1983	1984	1985	1986	1987
Terms of trade, food to non-food consumer goods	100	96	91	112	138	86	60	57	55
Relative prices, food to cocoa production	100	131	92	12	184	136	64	51	42

Source: John Loxley (1988).

Foreign trade and the balance of payments

The adjustment measures have been geared toward enhancing export production. Traditional exports such as cocoa, minerals, and timber have benefited as the terms of trade have shifted in their favour. Various lines of credit have been opened for reviving cocoa production and mining, and output therefrom has responded positively. So, despite the steady decline in international commodity prices, the country's export earnings have been increasing since 1983.

Attempts at diversifying Ghana's exports have not been so successful. Only a few non-traditional products such as pineapples, aubergines and veneer have found their way onto the world market. Cocoa remains the predominant export crop.

Imports have been increasing since 1983, resulting in persistent deficits in the balance of trade and payments (Table 2.4). Increased foreign aid promoted this situation, and the country did need imported spare parts to rehabilitate its industries and raw materials to make them operational. But because of trade liberalization the nation also now imports a large amount of finished consumer goods, and is building up a potential new debt burden for the future.

Table 2.4. Ghana, foreign trade balances, 1980–7 (in millions of US dollars)

	1980	1981	1982	1983	1984	1985	1986	1987
Current accounts balance	–55	508	–158	–230	–214	–264	–204	–224
Merchandise balance	132	–310	10	–100	–114	–96	–56	–198
Total exports	1104	711	641	439	567	632	749	827
Total imports	972	1021	631	539	681	729	805	1012

Source: World Bank (1989b).

Fiscal performance

The fiscal discipline introduced by the adjustment measures has yielded a number of budgetary surprises. The first surplus since independence was registered in 1986, and surpluses have persisted since. This is the result of policies aimed at eliminating inflationary pressures due to excessive government borrowing from the banks. Such policies have included the removal of subsidies on most consumer goods, including petroleum products; an increase in stumpage fees and royalties; the removal of some subsidies to higher education; the introduction of fees in the health sector; and the stepped-up efficiency of tax collection. By 1988 revenue had increased to about 14.5 per cent of GDP, from a level of only 5.5 per cent in 1983. The main sources included increased cocoa taxation, improved collection from companies, and rationalization of the sales and excise tax structures. Spending was restrained, declining from 11.9 per cent of GDP in 1986 to 10.5 per cent in 1988.

Prices and inflation

When adjustment measures were initiated in 1983, the inflation rate stood at 123 per cent. Within a year it had dropped to 40 per cent and by 1985 – after the bumper harvest that followed the good rains of the previous year – it went down to 10.3 per cent. Since then it has climbed somewhat, averaging 35 per cent yearly.

Ghana's inflation was thought of by both the IMF and the World Bank as a monetary phenomenon. Government had been financing its budgetary deficit through borrowing from the banking system, with money supply increasing at an average of 35 per cent per annum between 1972 and 1983 (despite a legal upper limit of 15 per cent set by the 1963 Bank of Ghana Act). Policies were implemented to put a squeeze on credit, but these do not seem to have slowed the expansion of the money supply. The new problem amounts to having swapped domestic credit for foreign credit. Even though the latter was secured on concessionary terms, new debt problems may arise in the long run. Meanwhile, inflation remains well above the target level of 10 per cent set for 1990.

The Social Consequences of Adjustment

Employment

Measurement difficulties and scarcity of data make it difficult to assess the effect of adjustment on labour. Figures from the 1984 population census and the 1987 Ghana Living Standards Survey (GLSS) indicate that unemployment as a percentage of labour force dropped from 2.8 per cent in 1984 to 1.9 per cent in 1987 (World Bank, 1989b: Table 12). These figures notwithstanding, certain of the adjustment policies are likely to have increased unemployment, at least in the urban areas.

Retrenchment and redeployment measures in the public sector were intended to prune the government payroll by some 60,000 by the end of 1989. The Ghana Cocoa Marketing Board (COCOBOD) and the Ghana Education Service have been the units most affected. The COCOBOD laid off 20,000 workers in 1985 and more since. More than 6000 were laid off by the education service in 1988. Other civil service sectors have been similarly shorn. These lay-offs affect urban areas the most and are likely to cause hardships in many households.

The government has counted on the retrenched workers being absorbed into the private workforce, as occurred after the 1983 repatriation from Nigeria, and that most will move into agriculture. Unfortunately, with the exception of cocoa, few incentives have been provided to encourage such employment. Moreover, private manufacturing in Ghana is not developed enough to absorb those retrenched from the public sector.

Adjustment is also bringing about vertical and horizontal shifts in the labour market. It has been observed that 'the ERP's reliance on market signals as means of achieving structural adjustment has been probably helped by a labour market sensitive to profitable opportunities' (Beaudry and Sowa, 1990). Evidence from the GLSS suggests that people have indeed moved into agriculture since adjustment began (Table 2.5). This may be a direct result of incentives provided to the cocoa sector through increases in producer prices, or a consequence of public-sector retrenchment, or both.

Table 2.5. Ghana, employment flows between economic sectors (1987–88)

	Origin (1)	Destination (2)	Net (2)–(1)
Farming	23.95	49.81	25.86
Forestry and mining	3.04	2.30	–0.76
Manufacturing	20.15	10.10	–10.01
Construction and transport	13.18	6.97	–6.21
Services	39.67	30.80	–8.87
	100%	100%	100%

Source: Beaudry and Sowa (1990): Table 5.4.

Prior to adjustment, migration was directed toward the urban areas, and especially toward Accra. After adjustment, the pattern reversed itself and Accra became a net source of out-migrants. Using GLSS data, Beaudry and Sowa observed that 'between 1982 and 1987, net migration out of Accra accounted for almost 60 percent of net outward migration in Ghana. The main destination of migrants has become the Western Region, which corresponds to the expanding cocoa production in that region' (Beaudry and Sowa, 1990).

Shifts in household earnings owing to adjustment measures have also affected employment. While living costs have increased, the nominal wage has remained abysmally low. The minimum nominal wage rate was doubled in 1985 from ₵35 per day to ₵70 per day, and there have been occasional further increases since then, but these have failed to maintain real wages at realistic levels. Indeed, estimates show that the average low-income family in Accra spends the equivalent of more than eight times the mininum wage. As a consequence, most salary-earners resort to second or third jobs to supplement earnings. Low real wages also drive people to illicit activity such as theft, corruption, black-marketeering, and prostitution.

Poverty profile

It has been observed that the adjustment process by its very nature inflicts severe short-run hardships on certain vulnerable groups (Kanbur, 1987). Ghana's experience has been no exception. Despite impressive macro-level growth statistics, both the absolute and relative levels of poverty increased among both the urban and rural populations during the adjustment period.

An Institute for African Development (IAD) special mission report estimated that the proportion of rural poor increased from 43 per cent in 1970 to 54 per cent in 1986. Other rough estimates showed that the number of urban dwellers below the poverty line increased from an average of 30–35 per cent in the late 1970s to between 45 and 50 per cent in the mid-1980s. The same study showed rural poverty to have increased from 60–65 per cent in the late 1970s to 67–72 per cent in the mid-1980s (Green, 1988). Thirty per cent and 10 per cent of the population, respectively, fall below the lines set by the World Bank of ₵31,552 per capita per year for 'poor' and ₵18,562 per capita per year for 'very poor'. The latter group has been termed the 'hard core poor' (Boateng et al., 1990). GLSS data indicate that about 19.2 per cent of the latter live in urban areas while 65.8 per cent live in rural areas, and the ratio is essentially the same for the ordinary poor. Taking into consideration that rural dwellers rely more on subsistence than on monetary income, the situation may well be grimmer for the urban poor. Those most likely to fall into the 'hard core' group in cities are the ones working in the so-called informal sector. These persons have been marginalized by adjustment policies that have resulted in high living costs relative to incomes. The majority of those in the 'hard core' poverty class are non-cocoa farmers; no 'white collar' workers fall into this category (Table 2.6).

Table 2.6. Ghana, distribution of the poor by occupation of head of household (1987–88)

Occupation	Poorest 10%	Poorest 30%	All Ghana
Cocoa farmer	5.7	17.5	18.4
Other farmer	79.6	61.7	44.5
Sales/services	3.0	4.2	10.9
Production/crafts	8.7	10.3	13.3
White collar	0.0	3.0	9.1
Retired	2.2	1.6	1.6
Unemployed	0.8	1.7	2.2

Source: World Bank /UNDP (1989).

PAMSCAD: mitigating the social costs

In order to address the plight of those adversely affected by the adjustment programme, the government instituted a Programme of Actions to Mitigate the Social Costs of Adjustment (PAMSCAD). Those targeted include rural households, low-income underemployed and unemployed urban households, and retrenched workers who lack productive employment.

Some of the interventions suggested under the programme include income and nutrition supplements. Projects chosen are selected on the basis of having a strong poverty focus and high social and economic rates of return. These include 'community initiative projects' as well as 'employment generation projects'. In addition there are projects designed to meet basic needs (water and sanitation, health care, nutrition, and shelter) for vulnerable groups. PAMSCAD is also intended to minimize the increased costs to parents due to the removal of subsidies in secondary schools (see below).

Implementation of projects under PAMSCAD has been slow owing to delays by donors in disbursing the US$84 million pledged in 1988 to initiate the programme.

Health and Education

Education and health care are vital indicators of the social achievements of a nation, but paucity of data precludes a full and objective analysis of these for Ghana. Overall, the country's situation has improved only slightly, and in some instances has become worse. The social infrastructure has run down over the years, and the quality of coverage and services provided in both education and health has deteriorated. The SAP thus targeted both these areas for 'adjustment'. But the principal change has involved the institution of full cost-recovery procedures for these and other public utilities, something that is expected to have a negative impact on access, particularly in the rural areas.

Improved sanitation and an increase in the number of medical facilities raised life expectancy at birth from 44.8 years in 1960 to 54 years in 1987. This came despite an increase in the patient : physician ratio owing to emigration of skilled personnel. This ratio increased from 13,740 : 1 in 1965 to 14,890 : 1 in 1984.

In education, the situation has clearly worsened since independence. The percentage of the primary school age population enrolled declined from 69 per cent in 1965 to 63 per cent in 1986. In secondary and tertiary education there was a slight improvement.

Health care

Prior to the adjustment measures, the health sector was financed mainly out of the national budget. Expenditures dropped sharply in the early 1980s, from 6.43 per cent of budget and 0.95 per cent of GDP in 1980 to 4.38 per cent and 0.35 per cent respectively in 1983. The government introduced hospital fees in July 1985 in an effort to recover part of the costs. By 1987, such fees constituted 13 per cent of the recurrent budget of the Ministry of Health. Service charges per outpatient varied regionally from ₵56 to ₵293. Cost recovery from drugs reaped about 34 per cent of the value of items dispensed.

Introduction of fees has been a disincentive to the use of health services. Declining hospital attendance before 1984 can be attributed to the overall crisis of the economy, but the continued drop through 1986 was due to the introduction of fees (Table 2.7). In some rural areas, outpatient attendance dropped by nearly 50 per cent. On average, 48 per cent of all sick Ghanaians did not consult a health provider of any kind, according to the 1987–8 GLSS.

In 1988, a policy was instituted whereby drugs deemed 'essential' are exempt from import duties. Yet such drugs cost so much in the first place that many outpatients

Table 2.7. Ghana, outpatient attendances, 1976–87

Year	Population (millions)	Outpatient attendances (millions)	Outpatient attendances per capita
1976	10.0	10.7	1.07
1980	10.7	6.3	0.59
1981	11.1	5.4	0.49
1982	11.5	6.2	0.54
1983	11.9	4.7	0.39
1984	12.3	4.5	0.37
1985	12.7	4.1	0.32
1986	13.2	4.2	0.32
1987	13.6	4.8	0.35

Source: World Bank (1989a): 73.

Table 2.8. Ghana, primary school enrolment, 1980–8

Year	Enrolment	% Change	Average annual growth rate (%)
1980/1	1,377,734	–	–
1981/2	1,533,859	12.0	12.78
1982/3	1,461,635	–6.12	–5.93
1983/4	1,452,458	–0.63	–0.63
1984/5	1,464,642	0.83	0.83
1985/6	1,325,485	–9.98	–9.50
1986/7	1,467,074	10.15	10.68
1987/8	1,535,505	4.56	4.66

Source: Ministry of Education; GSS, Quarterly Digest of Statistics, June 1989.

cannot afford them. Others simply visit dispensaries and pharmacy shops in order to avoid consultation fees.

There have been discussions about promoting primary health care, but very little has been done. Traditional birth attendants (TBA) are being trained in basic hygiene and first aid to enable them to offer improved services in the rural areas.

Table 2.9. Ghana, health expenditures, 1980–8

Year	% Share of of GDP	% Share of budget	Expenditures per capita (1984 cedis)
1980	0.95	6.43	258
1981	0.71	6.09	179
1982	0.62	6.09	141
1983	0.35	4.38	74
1984	0.84	8.50	184
1985	1.07	8.74	240
1986	1.15	8.28	260
1987*	1.20	7.40	282
1988*	1.40	8.50	323

* Includes project aid.
Source: World Bank (1989a).

Table 2.10. Ghana, education and the poor, 1987–8

Education of head of household	Poorest 10%	Poorest 30%	All Ghana
None	80.8	71.7	53.9
Primary	3.5	6.9	8.1
Middle	15.7	20.6	31.3
Secondary:			
O-Level	0.0	0.0	3.0
A-Level	0.0	0.0	0.3
Teacher training	0.0	0.5	1.8
Other post-secondary	0.0	0.3	0.4
University	0.0	0.0	1.2
School attendance:			
Ages 6–10	43.2	57.2	66.8
Ages 11–15	46.0	60.5	70.8

Source: World Bank, 1988.

Education

Drastic reforms have been made in education in Ghana since the adjustment programme began. While these were first announced in 1986, they were based on a 1974 commission report on 'The Structure and Content of Education'. The aims stated are the following:

1   to reduce the length of pre-university education from seventeen to twelve years;

2   to improve the quality of educational standards;
3   to contain and partially recover educational costs; and
4   to enhance sector management and budgeting procedures.

Under the recovery programme, the reforms have come in two phases and have been supported with funds from an Education Sector Adjustment Credit (EdSAC). The first phase (1987–90) concentrated on 'basic education' during the first nine years of schooling. Phase Two (1991–3) is to focus on senior secondary education. The following steps have been taken, mainly with an eye to finances:

1   *Redeployment:* Non-teaching and unqualified teaching staff have been redeployed from the education service and replaced almost one-for-one with qualified teachers, mainly returnees from Nigeria;
2   *Fee increases:* All pupils from grades three to nine are being charged book-user fees of ₡120 per pupil per year. In the secondary schools the book-user fees have been increased from ₡24 to ₡1500. When Phase Two of the programme is implemented, it is expected that new senior secondary students will pay the full costs of book use; at 1989 prices, between ₡2500 and ₡3000 per student per year. Besides these fee increases, exercise books that were once provided gratis are now being sold to students. All kinds of additional levies and charges are being demanded of parents, even for the construction of classrooms and workshops.

At the tertiary level, a new loan scheme was introduced in 1989 whereby ₡50,000 per annum is provided in lieu of 'allowances' for food, books, and miscellaneous expenses. But this sum can hardly provide for a university student's needs. (Students in particular disciplines such as medicine and agriculture, as well as deserving students in other fields, still enjoy government bursaries and scholarships.)

Subsidies on student meals at the boarding secondary schools have been withdrawn. A moratorium has been declared on the establishment of new boarding schools, and the government has further required that 30 per cent of all intake in existing schools be day students.

The overall effect of the fee increases on the welfare of students and their families is not difficult to imagine. Incomes were already inadequate for family support. Where education subsidies had once made it possible for poor students to attend university, this is now largely precluded. Giving more people literacy and numeracy by stressing basic education makes sense, but it should not be done at the expense of higher education.

Further rationalization in the tertiary institutions is expected before release of the second tranche under the EdSAC agreement. A University Rationalization Committee has recommended removal of subsidies, retrenchment and redeployment of staff, a freeze on the hiring of new lecturers, and an increase in student/lecturer ratios. Many of these steps have already been implemented.

Removal of subsidies at the tertiary level was supposed to make more resources available for basic education. And indeed, prior to the reforms, allocations were skewed toward higher education, with nearly sixty times as much being spent on a university student as on a primary student. Since reforms got under way, primary enrolment has begun to grow (Table 2.8).

Not surprisingly, education levels appear to be important factors in Ghana's poverty profile. GLSS data show that more than 80 per cent of the poor, and more than 70 per cent of the extremely poor, lived in households in which the head had no education. Among the extremely poor, school enrolment is about 45 per cent for children aged six to fifteen. The figure is near 60 per cent for the less poor, but both these figures are lower than for the population as a whole. The policy implication is that raising the level of education can help lower the proportion of Ghanaians beneath the poverty line.

Summary and Recommendations

Ghana's economy has gone through several phases since independence. A brief period of what could be termed 'development without growth' was followed by several years of decline, culminating in the near-famine situation of 1983. Causes of this crisis included economic mismanagement, political instability and corruption, and declining terms of trade for Ghana's exports. Together, these factors drove the country to the brink of bankruptcy. Foreign-exchange shortages led to shortages of raw materials and spare parts, and in turn to shortages of consumer goods. The country's GDP declined during most of the 1970s and early 1980s, and inflation soared to three-digit levels.

The ERP helped to stabilize this decline. Inflation is now down to around 35 per cent, and the GDP has been recording positive growth rates. In fulfilling the terms of the adjustment agreement, the government's budget has been registering surpluses since 1986. Adjustments in the exchange rate of the Cedi have made foreign currency available to producers through the market mechanism and without cumbersome administrative processes. Price controls have been removed to eliminate artificial shortages caused by previous administrative measures for market clearing.

The adjustment programme has called for reorganization of the health and education sectors. Rehabilitation of health infrastructure and improved management of health resources are proceeding. Inasmuch as a larger percentage of the poor have no access to medical facilities whatsoever, subsidies provided for health care benefit mainly the non-poor. Under such an argument it makes sense for the programme to institute certain kinds of cost-recovery. Still, since some of the poor are also in the urban areas, some subsidies ought to be maintained with discriminatory targeting. While the government has announced that those who cannot afford it will still enjoy 'free' medical care, administration of such a policy breeds favouritism, nepotism, and corruption. Implementation of a projected health-insurance scheme has been delayed.

A quite drastic overhaul of the education system has taken place under the adjustment measures. Pre-university education has been shortened from seventeen years to twelve. Fees for book usage have increased sharply and subsidies on food and boarding have been withdrawn. Tuition remains free thus far in the public institutions. University students now receive loans rather than allowances for books and board.

There can be no doubt that the adjustment measures have brought some successes to Ghana. Lack of continuity in economic policy was one of the factors that led to the economy's decline, and this is the first time that any sort of consistent economic programme has been followed. At least with the ERP in place, it can be monitored for flaws and 'adjusted' to solve problems as they arise. Nonetheless, there are two concerns that have not been adequately addressed: the programme's long-term sustainability, and its social consequences.

Much of the economy's recent growth has come in the non-productive sector. For a developing country, a 30 per cent share of GDP for the service sector is too high. But liberalization has enabled services to grow faster than Ghana's principal sector, agriculture. Food production has not received any incentives at all. To the contrary, incentives provided to cocoa and other tradable commodities have drawn farmers away from food production. This may jeopardize the country's potential for food self-sufficiency. With world-market prices for its products continuing to decline, Ghana is not even earning enough from exports to bring in food imports.

Renewed availability of foreign exchange has made it possible for some Ghanaian industries to be rehabilitated. But lack of working capital and shortages of bank credit have slowed growth even in these industries. Trade liberalization has also brought stiff competition from imports. Local factories that cannot compete have been closed down. Government ought to be working through the banks to provide soft credit to local entrepreneurs in order to encourage private development of the industrial sector. The existence of viable industrial establishments for processing agricultural produce could provide an important forward linkage for the development of the latter.

Adjustment policies have been harsh on human development. Retrenchment of employees in the public sector has left many urban households with only one working parent. Living costs have risen faster than nominal wages. Most people have to hold down two or even three jobs in order to survive.

The most dangerous thing about the adjustment programme is the illusions it fosters. Some people have indeed benefited, and it is easy for its proponents and supporters to point to these elements of success. But those marginalized by the programme have been pushed to the brink of survival. The government should target this latter group in order to raise the social development of the country as a whole.

References

Naseem Ahmad (1970). *Deficit Financing, Inflation and Capital Formation.* Munich: Weltforum Verlag.

Paul Beaudry and Nii K. Sowa (1990). *Labour Markets in an Era of Adjustment: A Case Study of Ghana.* Washington, DC: World Bank.

W. Birmingham and I. Neustadt (1966). *A Study of Contemporary Ghana.* London: George Allen & Unwin.

E. O. Boateng et al. (1990). *A Poverty Profile for Ghana, 1987–88.* Washington, DC: World Bank, SDA Working Paper No.5.

Jean M. Due (1973). 'Development Without Growth – The Case of Ghana in the 1960s'. *Economic Bulletin of Ghana* 3(1): 3–15.

R. H. Green (1988). 'The Human Dimension as the Test of and a Means of Achieving Africa's Economic Recovery and Development'. Paper presented at Conference on Human Dimensions of Africa's Economic Recovery and Development, Khartoum, Sudan, 3–8 March.

G. K. Helleiner (1989). 'Structural Adjustment and Long-Term Development in Sub-Saharan Africa'.

Paper presented at a workshop on Alternative Development Strategies in Africa, Queen Elizabeth House, Oxford, December 1989.

Anthony G. Hopkins (1973). *An Economic History of West Africa*. London: Longman.

Institute for African Development (1988). 'Report of the Special Programming Mission to Ghana'. Report No. 0105-GH.

S. M. R. Kanbur (1987). 'Measurement of Alleviation of Poverty: With an Application to the Impact of Macroeconomic Adjustment'. *Staff Papers, International Monetary Fund*.

Tony Killick (1978). *Development Economics in Action*. London: Heinemann.

John Loxley (1988). *Ghana: Economic Crisis and the Long Road to Recovery*. Ottawa: The North-South Institute.

Republic of Ghana (1984–6). *Economic Recovery Programme*. Accra.

A. Sawyerr (1988). 'The Politics of Adjustment Policy'. Paper presented at Conference on Human Dimensions of Africa's Economic Recovery and Development, Khartoum, Sudan, 3–8 March.

UN–ECA (1989). *African Alternative Framework to Structural Adjustment Programmes for Socio-Economic Recovery and Transformation*, Addis Ababa.

UNICEF (1986). *Ghana: Adjustment Policies and Programmes to Protect Children and Other Vulnerable Groups*. Accra.

World Bank (1988). *Ghana: Living Standards Surveys, Preliminary Results 1988*. Social Dimensions of Adjustment Unit. Washington, DC: World Bank.

World Bank (1989a). *Ghana: Population, Health and Nutrition Sector Review*. Washington, DC: World Bank.

World Bank (1989b). *Ghana: Structural Adjustment for Growth*. Washington, DC: World Bank.

World Bank/UNDP (1989). *Africa's Adjustment and Growth in the 1980s*. Washington, DC: World Bank.

3 Kenya

F. M. Mwega & J. W. Kabubo

Introduction

Kenya has an economy based on the production of primary commodities, a population of 24 million and an average GDP per capita of about US$370 in 1992. The agricultural sector contributed an average 25.1 per cent and the manufacturing sector (involved largely in agro-processing) an average 11.0 per cent to GDP in 1984–8. The economic structure has not changed much since independence; although there has been a decline in the share of the agricultural sector (from 39.3 per cent of GDP in 1964–8), the manufacturing sector's contribution has remained virtually constant (9.8 per cent in 1964–8), while the contribution of the service sector has slightly increased.

The economy is open and the commodity trade ratio (imports plus exports as a proportion of GDP) averaged 43 per cent in 1984–8, down from 46.4 per cent in 1964–8. Coffee, tea and sisal are the dominant commodity exports. Tourism and petroleum products are also important sources of foreign exchange, even though the latter's contribution to foreign exchange earnings is small. For example, in 1990, the country had 800,000 recorded visitors and since 1987 tourism has overtaken coffee to become the country's main foreign exchange earner. The country processes imported petroleum products and then exports them. Other manufactures contribute very little (about 10 per cent) to export earnings.

The openness of the economy and the heavy reliance on a few primary products implies that the country is highly vulnerable to exogenous shocks that influence earnings in international markets. Studies have confirmed a close correlation between terms of trade and the real growth of the economy (Vandermoortele, 1985).

In the first decade after independence (1964–73), the country performed very well, with the real GDP registering an average annual growth rate of 6.5 per cent, the agricultural sector 4.2 per cent and the manufacturing sector 8.2 per cent. This rapid growth rate was mainly the result of land reform in which land was redistributed to smallholders who utilized it more intensively, of the extension of cultivated land for high-value cash crops and of industrialization based on an import-substitution strategy. Another important source of growth was the ability of the economy to sustain high levels of saving and investment. Since the mid-1960s, gross investment has been larger than 19 per cent of GNP, with much of this financed from domestic savings. The rapid growth of the economy was, however, offset by an annual population growth rate of over 3 per cent, which has resulted in an average per capita GDP growth of about 3.4 per cent.

The import-substitution strategy pursued in the first decade of independence had a drastic impact on the structure of imports. The share of consumer imports in total imports declined from an average 25 per cent in 1964–8 to about 16 per cent in 1974–88, while the share of intermediate and capital imports rose from 75 per cent in 1964–8 to about 84 per cent in 1974–88. This has made the demand for imports relatively inelastic, making the economy very vulnerable to unexpected shortfalls in the supply of foreign exchange.

Table 3.1. Macro-economic performance indicators in Kenya, 1969–90

	1969–1973	1974–1978	1979–1983	1984–1988	1989–1990
Economic growth and inflation					
Growth of real GDP (% p.a.)	8.3	4.5	4.5	4.2	4.8
Change in real per capita consumption (% p.a.)	4.4	2.0	–2.6	0.8	–
Rise in GDP deflator (% p.a.)	4.1	14.0	9.6	9.2	–
Rise in consumer prices (% p.a.)	5.1	12.4	11.8	8.9	11.5
Balance of payments					
Terms of trade index	113	114	88	86	74
Change in import volumes (% p.a.)	0.6	4.0	–9.8	6.9	–1.5
Current account as % GDP	–4.2	–6.8	–7.8	–3.4	–6.2
Basic balance as % GDP	0.2	–0.5	–2.1	0.1	–3.7
External reserves as months of imports	4.3	4.0	2.8	2.7	1.5
Investment and savings					
Gross domestic fixed capital formation as % GNP	21.8	22.4	22.2	19.8	–
Gross national saving as % GNP	17.9	17.5	18.3	18.4	–
Financial indicators					
Government borrowing from banking system as % GDP	0.7	1.6	1.5	1.7	2.4
Growth in M2 (% p.a.)	18.3	21.4	9.6	12.5	16.5
Growth in domestic credit (% p.a.)	21.0	22.0	11.5	13.7	16.8
Growth in credit to public sector (% p.a.)	83.0	32.0	23.5	16.8	26.5
Share of private sector in total domestic credit (%)	82	71	65	58	60

Source: Kenya, *Statistical Abstract and Economic Survey,* various issues.

Other macro-economic indicators (Table 3.1) during this first decade also indicated a healthy economy. For example, the average rate of inflation was low at 3.4 per cent, the external reserves exceeded the legally stipulated four months' worth of imports and the modest current account deficit was more than compensated for by net long-term capital inflows, resulting in a positive basic balance.

The economy performed less well in the 1974–90 period, as indicated by a lower average real growth rate of only 4 per cent, a high average inflation rate of 11 per cent and a less impressive external account. Foreign exchange reserves have been smaller than the stipulated four months' worth of imports in much of the period, while the current account deficit could not be compensated for by long-term net capital inflows.

Deterioration in economic performance can be traced to various adverse exogenous developments, inappropriate fiscal and monetary policies, especially in the early and late 1970s, and domestic structural factors, especially the failure to expand and diversify exports. Exogenous developments included the oil crises of 1973–4 and 1979–80 and the consequent world recession; increased protectionism in developed countries; high external interest rates and a decline in concessionary capital inflows; the droughts of 1974–5, 1979–80 and 1983–4, which adversely affected agricultural production and led to massive food imports; the breakdown of the East African Community in 1977, which significantly eroded the market for Kenya's non-traditional exports; and a military coup attempt in 1982, which adversely affected investment and caused some capital flight. By the close of the 1970s, economic observers were generally agreed that Kenya needed to institute major structural policy changes to stabilize the economy and to restore a reasonable rate of economic growth in the changed domestic and increasingly hostile international environment.

Structural Adjustment Programmes in Kenya

Kenya did not experience a major balance of payments problem in the 1960s and therefore did not seek loans from the international financial institutions (IFIs). The country experienced its first major external payments problem in 1971, when there was a drastic rundown of reserves following an experiment in expansionary fiscal policies. This problem was followed by the oil crisis of 1973–4. The government reacted to these crises by tightening the trade regime and seeking external finances whose general policy conditionalities were spelt out in official documents such as the 1974–8 Development Plan and the 1975 Sessional Paper No. 4 on Economic Prospects and Policies. Since then the country has used direct controls to ration foreign exchange.

The IMF programmes adopted in the early 1970s were abandoned when the country experienced an improvement in the balance of payments resulting from a large increase in the prices of coffee and tea in 1975–7, due to a frost in Brazil that drastically reduced its coffee harvest. The proceeds of this boom were fully passed on to the farmers. The resulting expansion in aggregate demand (coinciding with the second oil crisis of 1979–80) produced a serious balance of payments crisis beginning in 1978, which the government sought to contain through a restrictive trade policy. The external account problems again forced the country to seek loans from the IFIs.

Even though the IMF programmes negotiated in 1979–82 collapsed because the stipulated credit ceilings were exceeded, the government was able to successfully implement later programmes and has had programmes with the IMF since then, except in 1986–7. The 1980s were therefore a period when the country attempted fairly sustained stabilization, structural adjustment and economic liberalization efforts.

In this process Kenya received large external capital inflows for the financing of imports, consequently incurring a large external debt burden. The ratio of external debt to export earnings increased from 38.2 per cent in 1974 to 162.9 per cent in 1987. The external debt service charges, 3.0 per cent of export earnings in 1974, is now about a third of export earnings.

Sectoral structural adjustment programmes have been financed mainly by the World Bank. Kenya was one of the first African countries to qualify for a Structural Adjustment Loan from the World Bank in 1980, aimed at helping the economy correct economic imbalances and achieve some institutional reforms for a sustainable and balanced growth. The loan was to finance structural changes in the industrial sector, promote efficient use of external resources and enhance the effectiveness of public investment. In addition, the loan conditionalities required the country to reduce the budget deficit, change the manner of its financing towards non-inflationary means, liberalize trade, promote exports and reform the interest-rate regime.

In 1982, Kenya signed a second Structural Adjustment Loan intended to achieve similar objectives. The third Structural Adjustment Loan, in 1986, was to finance reforms in the agricultural sector in order to enhance production and investment incentives, and finance the importation of agricultural inputs and the improvement of agricultural research facilities. It was also intended to support parastatal reforms and aid the restructuring of the public investment and expenditure programme.

In 1988, another Structural Adjustment Loan was contracted to finance reforms in education and health. Agreed policies included 'cost sharing' whereby the beneficiaries of these social services were to pay for them, either partially or fully. They also included a reduction in public expenditure, with more support funds to come from the private sector. These policies were employed with some success. The government also reduced the rate of employment creation in the public sector in an effort to reduce public expenditure.

To encourage competition in the domestic industrial sector and create an enabling economic environment for the operation of market forces, price controls have been gradually lifted, particularly for non-essential consumer and producer goods. This was accompanied by the easing of non-price restrictions in the grain market, especially monopoly buying and distribution of such crops as maize. In the private sector, monopolistic practices are to be curtailed: towards this end, a Monopolies and Restrictive Practices Act was passed by parliament in 1990.

To make the industrial sector more competitive, the protection accorded the sector has been reduced through import tariffs and by a systematic dismantling of quantitative restrictions on imports. The Foreign Investment Protection Act was recently amended to encourage foreign investors, while action has been taken to cut red tape in the investment approval procedure. The Investment Promotion Centre was established in 1986 to assist potential investors through its Green Channel facility.

A number of incentives have been provided for exporters, especially of non-traditional products. These include an export compensation (subsidy) scheme for manufactured exports which has been in existence since 1974, manufacturing under bond and export processing zones. A crawling-peg exchange rate policy has been in effect since the early 1980s.

Numerous other sectoral structural adjustment policies have been partially implemented in the agricultural and financial sectors. Producer prices have been raised to induce farmers to increase output of foodstuffs. The producer prices are usually reviewed just before the planting season every year. Moreover, the timely supply of inputs is ensured and adequate agricultural credit is provided. In the financial sector, the central bank's supervisory role over commercial banks and non-bank financial intermediaries has been strengthened, while policies to promote saving and investment have been adopted. In the money and capital markets, discount markets were created and the stock exchange has been strengthened in order to improve the supply of long-term credit and equity.

The structural adjustment programmes have also covered public investment. New procedures and institutional mechanisms have been initiated, mostly through a budget rationalization programme started in 1986. The objective is to contain the growth in government expenditure and to reduce the budget deficit. Through this programme, the government would identify high-priority projects for additional funding and speedier implementation, and low-priority projects to be postponed or cancelled. Thereafter, it would ensure that recurrent resources are available in the future to operate and maintain completed priority projects and generally to improve the utilization of completed facilities.

The budget deficit was to be reduced through an increase in government tax revenue and appropriations-in-aid. Tax revenue was to be increased via improvement of tax administration and gradual reform of the tax structure. Non-tax revenue was to be boosted by the policy of charging some fees for public sector services, especially education and health.

Monetary policy in Kenya aims at containing inflation while ensuring an adequate credit supply consistent with a viable balance of payments. The principal monetary aggregate in the pursuit of this policy is M2 – currency outside banks plus commercial bank deposits. The growth in M2, for example, fell from 21.4 per cent in 1974–8 to 9.6 per cent in 1979–83, then rose slightly to 12.5 per cent in 1984–8. The government is trying to curtail its borrowing from the domestic banking system (which has been about 1.5 per cent of GDP since the mid-1970s) in an effort to reduce the financial crowding-out of the private sector.

In order to encourage the mobilization of savings, discourage unproductive investment and contribute towards financial stability, official policy seeks to maintain real interest rates at positive levels. Given a fairly high rate of inflation, this necessitates the maintenance of equally high nominal interest rates. As a consequence, the real deposit rates, which were less than –7.0 per cent in the 1970s, were increased to 2.3 per cent in 1986–90. Interest rates were fully freed from administrative controls in July 1991. This interest rate liberalization has been accompanied by a restructuring of the institutional framework within which commercial banks and non-bank financial institutions operate. The investment climate is being made more attractive, particularly for foreign investors, who provide about a third of the investment finance.

Effects of Structural Adjustment Programmes

These structural adjustment programmes have had numerous effects on the economy, such as inflationary pressures, marginalization of the poor in the distribution of educational and health benefits and reduction in employment. These effects are analysed below.

The budget deficit

One of the most important objectives of the structural adjustment policies has been to reduce the budget deficit. In the early independence years, management of the budget deficit was very successful. The government was able to respond to pent-up frustration from the colonial period by rapidly expanding education, health and other services while at the same time actually improving the overall situation and greatly reducing dependence on aid grants from the United Kingdom. There was a substantial and growing surplus in the current account budget from 1.5 per cent to 2.3 per cent of GDP in 1969–78.

The situation changed in the 1970s when the government's current account surplus became a deficit. Relative to GDP, the overall deficit grew after the mid-1970s and it became more difficult to avoid inflationary borrowing from the banking system, which rose from 0.7 per cent of GDP in 1969–73 to about 1.6 per cent in the mid-1980s. The high point of the budget deficit was reached in 1986–7 when it was equal to 9 per cent of GDP. Except for the coffee and tea boom of 1977–8, more than half of the budget deficits were financed from domestic sources.

Many of the planned reforms in government budgeting have to a large extent been implemented to bring the budget deficit under control. Government ministries have also since the early 1980s been required to submit to the Treasury their estimated revenue and expenditures based on an *a priori* review and approved forward budget (first instituted in 1986), and have been subject to expenditure ceilings. As a component of the budget rationalization exercise, line ministries were asked to ensure that only priority and unavoidable expenditures were included in their proposals to the treasury, with priorities designated so that adjustments could be made without resorting to across-board cuts. Ministries were advised that because of financial constraints, there would be no supplementary estimates for either recurrent or development expenditures.

Inadequate expenditure control has been an important part of the budgetary problem in Kenya: total government spending rose relative to economic activity from about 24 per cent of GDP in the late 1960s to an average of around 35 per cent in the late 1980s, with serious budget financing difficulties emerging in the late 1970s. According to the 1982–3 budget speech, there was severe deterioration in financial discipline within ministries, some of which treated the budgetary process as well as the planning and implementation of the development programme in a perfunctory manner despite Treasury instructions on expenditure control and other aspects of financial management.

Not the least of the difficulties here (Tables 3.2 and 3.3) is that the two main components of government spending are the salaries of the civil service (which account for nearly 70 per cent of recurrent spending) and the local currency costs of servicing

Table 3.2. Composition of central government expenditures

	Wages & salaries	Goods & services	GFKF%	Subsidies, transfers	Debt & service	Lending & investment	Total
1964–9	31.7	16.1	11.5	22.4	10.2	8.3	100
1969–74	35.5	17.1	18.8	11.1	9.2	8.5	100
1974–9	22.5	23.8	15.9	17.0	8.9	11.6	100
1979–83	18.9	27.3	14.8	17.6	14.8	6.6	100
1983–4	21.3	26.5	9.6	17.6	14.8	6.6	100
1984–5	18.9	20.8	12.7	20.4	24.9	2.4	100
1985–6	20.4	21.5	9.1	19.5	26.5	3.1	100
1986–7	19.1	19.9	13.6	21.4	23.7	2.3	100
1987–8	20.4	21.8	10.9	20.8	24.8	1.3	100
1988–9	18.4	17.8	12.7	16.3	32.7	2.1	100
1989–90*	17.6	18.5	14.2	17.5	30.2	2.0	100
1990–1*	15.6	20.9	14.0	16.7	31.8	1.0	100

Source: Kenya, Economic Survey, various issues.
* Provisional

Table 3.3. Composition of central government expenditures by function

	General administration %	Economic services %	Social services* %	Others** %	Total %	Total K£ mn
1975–6	19.5	33.3	35.0	12.0	100	373.11
1976–7	15.3	31.6	40.9	12.2	100	409.76
1977–8	15.6	32.4	39.2	12.8	100	590.39
1978–9	14.2	33.5	40.1	12.2	100	697.61
1979–80	16.3	27.9	42.4	13.4	100	781.32
1980–1	17.0	29.6	38.1	15.3	100	962.11
1981–2	15.1	27.6	39.1	18.2	100	1122.32
1982–3	11.7	22.9	38.5	26.9	100	1190.68
1983–4	13.0	24.3	38.3	24.4	100	1242.43
1984–5	14.0	25.9	34.0	26.1	100	1483.23
1985–6	13.9	26.3	33.4	26.4	100	1534.66
1986–7	12.5	22.6	37.0	27.9	100	1655.73
1987–8	13.8	19.2	40.9	26.1	100	2227.55
1988–9	13.3	20.4	32.7	33.6	100	2966.70
1989–90	14.7	20.3	33.6	31.4	100	3157.10
1990–1	13.5	20.5	32.9	33.1	100	3996.63

Source: Kenya, Economic Survey, various issues.
* Education, health, housing and welfare and defence
** Includes public debt.

the public debt – a cost which has been mounting as a result of the depreciation of the Kenya shilling. There has been a decrease in the share of subsidies and transfers as well as in development expenditures. The shares of expenditure on administration and on economic and social services seem to have declined despite the inclusion of defence expenditures.

Impact of structural adjustment policies on the education sector

Kenya has made remarkable progress in the education sector in quantitative terms, such as increases in the number of educational institutions and enrolments. There are several problems in the sector, however, which led the World Bank to advise cost-sharing schemes and a reduction of government expenditures on social services. These problems include: high drop-out rates from schools; limited access to education in disadvantaged areas; low enrolment rates and a significant drop in adult literacy classes. Moreover, the Ministry of Education's expenditure's have been rising to formidable levels. The share of recurrent expenditure on education in Kenya out of the total recurrent expenditure more than doubled from about 15 per cent in the 1960s to 30 per cent in 1980 and 35 per cent in 1987. It was therefore found necessary to institute measures to reduce recurrent expenditure to enable the government to expand and improve existing educational institutions.

In 1979–80, the recurrent expenditure on education was K£114.9 million while K£11.0 million was spent on investment. Primary education received the largest share, accounting for 65 per cent of the total recurrent expenditure. Recurrent expenditure rose to K£229.9 million in 1984–5 while development expenditure was only K£10.9 million. The introduction of the 8.4.4 educational system in 1984 to replace the 7.6.3 system increased recurrent expenditure by approximately 30 per cent in 1985–6 over

Table 3.4. Expenditure on education 1980–91, K£ million

Year	Recurrent	Development
1980–1	148.93	10.62
1981–2	165.97	11.26
1982–3	177.55	10.19
1983–4	194.89	10.44
1984–5	229.85	10.90
1985–6	295.44	11.12
1986–7	336.27	21.14
1987–8	404.02	23.41
1988–9	450.02	36.76
1989–90	489.77	36.63
1990–1	529.77	95.79

Source: Kenya, Economic Survey, various issues.
Figures for 1990–1 are estimates.

1984–5. Primary education continued to receive the largest share of development expenditure in the 1985–6 financial year.

Development expenditure is estimated to have tripled in 1990–1 over 1989–90 due to the increased intake of students in the four public universities (Table 3.4). The share of recurrent education expenditure in the national recurrent budget rose from 25.6 per cent in 1978–9 to 37.7 per cent in 1987–8 (Table 3.5).

The proposed cost-sharing measures were designed to deal with the problems of the disproportionately large share of the recurrent budget, increased enrolment and reduced quality of education, and insufficient funds for books and equipment. First, a large part of the burden of educating children even at the primary level was to be

Table 3.5. Share of recurrent education expenditure in the national recurrent budget (KSh million)

Year	Education (1)	Growth rate %	National recurrent budget (2)	Growth rate %	1 as % of 2
1978–9	1907.5	3.7	7439.6	15.3	25.6
1979–80	2293.9	20.3	7945.4	6.8	28.8
1980–1	2977.1	30.7	10120.2	27.4	29.6
1981–2	3298.2	10.0	11006.0	8.8	29.6
1982–3	3548.6	7.6	11658.0	5.9	30.4
1983–4	3671.1	3.5	12251.7	5.1	29.9
1984–5	4426.8	20.6	14825.6	21.0	29.8
1985–6	5926.8	33.8	16529.6	11.5	35.8
1986–7	6760.1	14.0	18593.8	12.5	36.4
1987–8	7711.7	14.6	23338.2	25.5	37.7
Average growth rate		16.8		14.0	

Source: Odada and Odhiambo (1989): 110.

Table 3.6. Enrolment in educational institutions 1979–89

Year	Primary	Secondary	Technical institutions	University
1979	3698196	384389	13442	7292
1980	4926629	399389	13784	7631
1981	3980763	409850	14734	7588
1982	4184602	438344	15674	–
1983	4323921	493710	17914	7418
1984	4380232	510943	19123	7330
1985	4702414	401978	19826	7608
1986	4843423	458712	21093	9377
1987	4957700	514300	18131	18883
1988	4985400	553200	17855	26000
1989	4994300	734700	19512	29900

Source: Odada and Odhiambo (1989): 109.

borne by parents, who were to pay fees and buy books, uniforms and so on. Second, parents were to contribute to the building of schools through *harambee* (self-help) contributions.

Through cost-sharing, it has been possible for the government to provide more and better educational services than would otherwise be the case. This has resulted in a steady increase in enrolments in educational institutions from primary to university level (Table 3.6).

The number of primary schools rose from 10,255 in 1980 to 14,864 in 1990, while the number of secondary schools increased from 1785 to 2678. Furthermore, while the number of primary teacher training colleges (17) did not change, existing colleges have been upgraded and new ones established in their place. The number of secondary teacher training colleges increased from 4 to 7.

Nevertheless, the direct impact of structural adjustment programmes on the society may be seen at the primary level, where cost-sharing has hiked school fees. Though initial enrolments are high, many children tend to drop out of primary school before they reach Standard Eight due to lack of funds for activity fees, building funds, books and uniforms. The same effect is felt at the secondary school level: some students who qualify for Form One do not enrol due to lack of funds. This leads eventually to children from well-to-do families taking up educational opportunities at higher levels at the expense of their counterparts from poor families. Thus, cost-sharing tends to marginalize the poor by offering opportunities to only those who can afford to pay, thereby promoting social inequality in the country.

The effects of cost-sharing schemes may also have a negative impact on students from less well-off backgrounds at public universities. Cost reduction measures proposed for the universities include reduction of student allowances by half, implementation of which has prompted a proposal that undergraduate students be admitted as day students due to the universities' limited boarding facilities; encouragement of the admission of self-sponsored students in the public universities; discontinuation of students' personal allowances in public universities and colleges; management by commercial banks of the student loan schemes; and payment of the full cost of accommodation by students in public education and training institutions, including universities.

The long-term effect of such cost-sharing measures on training institutions and universities is likely to be a decline in the number of students. At present, many students cannot afford to pay the fees charged in teacher-training and other diploma colleges. Many university students may find it difficult to raise the required fees and to meet their accommodation expenses. An individual cost benefit analysis of university education may therefore discourage students from attending universities given the current state of graduate unemployment in the country.

The untimely increase in the number of training institutions and enrolments has resulted in a major crisis in the educational system. The quality of education has declined in the face of limited facilities.

Impact of adjustment measures on employment

Wage employment in the Kenyan economy expanded steadily over the years, but given the high population growth rate, many new job-market entrants have remained unemployed. In 1980, growth in total wage employment was estimated at 3.4 per cent, but a total of 260,100 job seekers had registered themselves as unemployed with the Ministry of Labour. The growth rate dropped in 1981 and 1982 due to a general decline in investment in the private sector. Public sector wage employment also decreased in agriculture and forestry, building and construction, and communication.

The rate of growth was highest in 1988 due to the launching of the Nyayo tea zones as an agro-corporation. Thereafter the rate of growth declined to 4.4 per cent in 1989, rising marginally to 4.5 per cent in 1990, to result in total employment of 1.889 million (Table 3.7).

Structural adjustment programmes have adversely affected employment in the public sector, the largest source of employment in Kenya. The Budget Rationalization Programme aims for: (1) a slower growth rate of employment in the public sector; (2) the engagement of additional staff by local authorities only when this contributes to expanded services; (3) reduction of public sector employment through divestiture of non-strategic activities; and (4) a public sector training policy in which trainees will not automatically be absorbed into government employment but will compete for entry, with some going into self-employment or wage-employment in the private sector.

Given limited expansion of employment opportunities, even university and college graduates have joined the unemployed. The labour force is expected to grow from an estimated 8.6 million in 1988 to 10.6 million in 1993, while total modern sector employment is expected to grow at the rate of 4.2 per cent annually from an estimated 1.37 million in 1988 to 1.68 million in 1993. This implies that about 8.92 million people will have to find jobs in the informal sector or remain unemployed in 1993.

Table 3.7. Persons engaged in 1980–90 in thousands

| Year | Modern establishment[1] | | Informal sector | Total |
	wage employees	self-employed[2]		
1980	1005.8	61.9	123.1	1190.8
1981	1024.3	62.1	157.3	1243.7
1982	1046.0	62.7	172.2	1280.9
1983	1093.0	63.2	182.9	1339.4
1984	1119.7	32.4	197.8	1349.9
1985	1174.4	33.4	254.5	1462.0
1986	1220.5	35.4	281.1	1537.0
1987	1264.5	38.1	312.1	1614.7
1988	1341.3	43.9	346.2	1731.4
1989	1372.8	44.3	390.8	1807.1
1990[3]	1407.7	48.2	443.1	1889.0

Source: Kenya, Economic Survey, various issues.
Notes: 1 Rural and urban areas
        2 Self employed and unpaid family workers
        3 Figures for 1990 are estimates.

Impact of adjustment measures on the health sector

Over the 1980s, Kenya pursued the objective of providing health for all by the year 2000, by increasing the number of health institutions in the country and training more medical personnel.

The number of registered doctors almost doubled from 1691 in 1980 to about 3357 in 1990, thereby increasing the number of doctors per 10,000 population from approximately 10 to 14. Other medical personnel have also increased steadily with the most remarkable increase being for enrolled nurses (Table 3.8).

Table 3.8. Registered medical personnel – selected years

	1980	1983	1987	1990*
Doctors	1691	2514	3071	3357
Dentists	162	289	492	596
Pharmacists	60	113	362	443
Pharmaceutical technologists	229	395	494	604
Registered nurses	6692	8547	9862	5441
Enrolled nurses	8722	10168	13202	17734
Clinical officers	1681	1921	2355	2630

Source: Kenya, Economic Survey, various issues.
* Provisional

Similarly, the number of health institutions increased considerably from 1544 in 1980 to 2131 in 1989, while the number of hospital beds and cots increased from 27,691 to 32,534 (Table 3.9). However, the number of beds and cots per 100,000 population dropped from 174 in 1980 to 136 in 1989, implying that the increase in beds and cots did not match the rate of population growth. Government had to increase funds allocated to the health sector, which now accounts for approximately 6 per cent of government gross expenditure. However, the larger proportion of the sector's expenditure was recurrent (Table 3.10). The relationship between recurrent and development expenditure of the Ministry of Health changed very little over the years.

Gross expenditure on the sector as a proportion of gross government expenditure actually declined from 7 per cent in 1980 to 6 per cent in 1986. Such funding is grossly inadequate for the health sector and needs to be increased.

Health care financing raises a number of issues: the relative decrease and inadequacy of public revenue; increasing demand for health services; recurrent expenditure and revenue gaps; and the impact on services and service delivery. There are several weaknesses in health financing which include a revenue generation crisis, a growing gap between financial resource requirements of a project and proposed resource availability from public budgetary sources, and underfunding of existing health services resulting in a drop in effectiveness.

Due to the inadequacy of funds exacerbated by the high population growth rate, the government had to adopt cost-sharing schemes: increased contributions to the mandatory health insurance fund for wage workers; fees charged for public inspection and community participation in training institutions; and maintenance of community

Table 3.9: Health institutions and hospital beds and cots

	Health institutions				Hospital beds & cots	
Year	Hospitals	Health Cs	Health Cs, Sc	Total	Beds & Cots	No. per 100,000
1980	216	241	1087	1544	27,691	174
1981	221	262	1130	1613	28,108	177
1982	220	276	1135	1631	29,044	171
1983	216	228	1213	1717	29,294	· 156
1984	213	229	1273	1779	30,886	158
1985	243	269	1173	1683	30,936	153
1986	249	276	1424	1959	31,356	148
1987	254	282	1553	2071	31,356	146
1988	260	294	1553	2107	31,983	141
1989	268	299	1564	2131	32,534	136

Source: Kenya, Economic Survey, various issues.
Notes: Cs stands for centres
Sc stands for sub-centres.

health institutions and contribution, through amenity wards in public hospitals. The government levied charges for out-patient services as well as increased public health service charges. The former measure was implemented for some time, but was later scrapped.

The sixth Development Plan (1989–93) noted that in order to achieve the objective of health for all by the year 2000, cost effectiveness has to be achieved. This, it is argued, would promote health awareness by leading individuals and communities to take greater responsibility for their own health, with a greater role of achieving that objective being played by the private sector, self-help groups and non-governmental organizations. Moreover, drugs are to be provided at cost in public facilities.

The impact of such measures in the health sector is severest on the poor, who cannot afford to pay for health services. For example, when the government introduced the payment of 20 shillings for all new out-patient cases, many people had to forgo treatment in public facilities, a situation which resulted in the scrapping of the scheme.

Table 3.10. Recurrent and development expenditure as a proportion of total gross expenditure in the Ministry of Health

Year	Recurrent expend. (%)	Development expend. (%)	Gross expend. on health as a % of GE
1980	80.26	19.74	7.0
1981	80.58	19.42	6.7
1982	84.11	15.89	6.3
1983	89.01	10.99	5.9
1984	84.88	15.12	5.9
1985	87.54	12.46	5.4
1986	87.17	17.83	6.0

Source: Odada and Odhiambo (1989): 81.

The situation is further aggravated by a severe shortage of drugs in government health institutions, forcing patients to meet the extra cost of purchasing them from private pharmacies.

Other adjustment measures that have an impact on the health sector include devaluation of the Kenya shilling, cuts in public spending, high taxation on mass consumption goods, removal of subsidies on basic foodstuffs and other basic needs, removal of price controls and improvement in public sector planning and execution.

These measures have both positive and negative effects on the delivery of health care services. Devaluation increased the domestic prices of imported goods such as drugs and medical equipment, increased the cost of health inputs (e.g., clean and safe water), and led to inflation. However, it had the positive effect of stimulating exports, hence raising incomes and employment. This in turn may reduce poverty and improve the health status of the population.

Cuts in public spending have led to a reduction in training funds, thus reducing the number of trained personnel. They have also reduced funds for buying drugs, vaccines and other medical supplies, and have limited the ability of the Ministry of Health to employ more health manpower, thereby inhibiting further improvement of the ratios of health personnel to population. Lastly, they have reduced funds for preventive and promotive health interventions. High taxation of mass consumption goods has the negative effect of slowing down self-training of personnel and reduces the welfare of poor households. Removal of subsidies reduces access to food, thus exacerbating malnutrition and poor housing. However, on the positive side, cuts in public spending, taxation of mass consumption goods, and the removal of subsidies have tended to reduce government deficits and debt, and to lower inflation. This may increase the purchasing power of the population, release resources for development expenditure and capital formation for further economic growth, and, potentially, save or generate more government revenue for increased expenditures on health.

However, the removal of price controls has the negative impact of causing an additional burden on vulnerable groups because of the tendency of prices to escalate, although it may also create incentives for more production and employment, at least in the medium term.

Improvement in public sector planning and execution could increase the efficiency of health care delivery, thereby saving on resource inputs and enhancing the quality of health care services. Unfortunately, such improvement in public sector planning has not been achieved in Kenya. The overall effect of structural adjustment programmes on the health sector has therefore been a reduction in household savings, since an increased proportion of the consumer's income is devoted to paying for health care.

Conclusions

In this chapter we have reviewed the socio-economic implications of structural adjustment policies typically recommended by the World Bank. The adoption of these policies has been to a large extent influenced by adverse macro-economic developments especially in the 1980s, which led Kenya to seek high conditionality loans from IFIs. The policies have covered education, health, employment and trade. The main objective of the policies was to reduce the budget deficit by scaling down government expenditure and by increasing the taxation of benefits through more widespread use of users' fees.

We have discussed the impact of adjustment measures on employment, education and health sectors. The direct effects of structural adjustment programmes in the education sector is reflected in a massive increase in school fees and other charges, a reduction in the quality of educational programmes, and an increase in the number of drop-outs from the school system. This skews access to education opportunities away from the poor, marginalizes them and may eventually worsen social inequalities.

Structural adjustment measures in the health sector have also adversely affected the poor, who can barely afford the fees needed to pay for services. The situation is aggravated by lack of drugs in government health institutions. The policy choice may then be to charge fees and improve the quality of services offered by public health facilities. The health sector has been affected by, among other policies, devaluation of the Kenya shilling, high taxation of goods, removal of subsidies on basic foodstuffs and other basic needs.

The public sector is the largest employer in Kenya. Structural adjustment programmes have adversely affected employment and earnings in the sector. With limited expansion of the private sector, graduates from universities and colleges remain unemployed over long periods. At the same time the decline in real wages since the mid-1970s has reduced the productivity (and morale) of the civil service.

References and Bibliography

A. B. Ayako and J. E. O. Odada. (1988). *The Impact of Structural Adjustment Policies on the Well-being of the Vulnerable Groups in Kenya.* Nairobi: UNICEF.

B. Balassa (1982). 'Structural Adjustment Policies in Developing Economies'. *World Development,* Vol. 10, No. 1.

— (1984). *Adjustment Policies in Developing Countries: A Reassessment.* Washington: World Bank, Development Research Department.

Government of Kenya (1986). *Sessional Paper No. 1 of 1986 on Economic Management for Renewed Growth.* Nairobi: Ministry of Planning and National Development.

— (1988). *Sessional Paper No. 6 of 1988 on Education and Manpower Training for the Next Decade and Beyond.* Nairobi: Ministry of Education.

— *Development Plan,* various issues. Nairobi: Ministry of Planning and National Development.

— *Economic Survey,* various issues. Nairobi: Government Printer.

— *Statistical Abstract,* various issues. Nairobi: Government Printer.

J. E. O. Odada and L. O. Odhiambo (1989). *Report of the Proceedings of the Workshop on Cost-Sharing in Kenya.* Naivasha-Kenya.

J. Vandermoortele (1985). 'Causes of Economic Instability in Kenya: Theory and Evidence'. *Eastern Africa Economic Review,* Vol 1, No. 1.

World Bank (1981). *Accelerated Development in Sub-Saharan Africa: An Agenda for Action.* Washington.

— (1983). 'Student Loans as a Means of Financing Higher Education'. Washington: World Bank Staff Working Papers No. 599.

— (1984). 'Adjustment Policies in Developing Countries'. Washington: World Bank Staff Working Papers, No. 675.

— (1984). 'Controlling the Cost of Education in Eastern Africa. A Review of Data Issues and Policies'. Washington: World Bank, Staff Working Papers, No. 702.

__ (1984). *Towards Sustained Development in Sub-Saharan Africa. A Joint Programmes for Action.* Washington.

— (1988). *Education in Sub-Saharan Africa: Policies for Adjustment, Revitalization and Expansion.* Washington.

4 Sierra Leone

Josie W. Eliott

Economy and Policy in the 1980s Crisis

The government of Sierra Leone has on a number of occasions since 1966 had recourse to the structural adjustment lending facilities of the International Monetary Fund. Under such loans, the IMF calls for both stabilization and adjustment measures. The former, aimed at an immediate balancing of revenue and expenditures, typically entail the streamlining of government finances, the liberalization of domestic markets, increasing real interest rates, stimulating gross capital formation through domestic mobilization of credit, enhancing international credit-worthiness, and, perhaps most importantly, the use of currency devaluation or depreciation measures (Taylor, 1988). Adjustment measures, on the other hand, involve new investment strategies geared toward increasing levels of production and productivity over the medium to long term. In real life, these two sets of measures are inextricably linked, and it is difficult to disentangle their impacts on the economy as a whole.

The IMF model assumes a highly flexible economy susceptible to smooth adjustment. This is a problematic notion at best for the countries of sub-Saharan Africa, where the economies are highly fragmented and remain concentrated on monocultural exports of agricultural goods and unprocessed minerals. In the case of Sierra Leone, subsistence farming continues to predominate, with a low level of output: while 65 per cent of the labour force is engaged in agriculture, this sector contributes only 35 per cent of Gross National Product. Production of rice, the staple food crop, meets only 70 per cent of domestic demand. Cocoa, coffee, and palm kernels constitute the principal export crops. While diamond mining was long a key sector, it has declined owing to the depletion of alluvial deposits and the failure to shift into more capital-intensive kimberlite mining. The small manufacturing sector is largely geared towards import substitution. Infrastructure is inadequate, and development of human resources has been limited: life expectancy is only 38 years; infant mortality is 200 per 1000 live births; and the literacy rate is 15 per cent, among the lowest in the world. Skilled personnel at the middle and lower levels of public administration are in short supply.

Nonetheless, Sierra Leone's economy managed to achieve a 5 per cent annual growth during the first decade of independence (up to 1972), largely on the basis of mineral exports and relatively favourable terms of trade for agricultural commodities. Even after the first round of oil-price hikes, real economic growth remained above 3 per cent annually until 1975 and fell only to just under 2 per cent between 1975 and 1980. Decline set in seriously during 1980–3, as agricultural and mineral output fell and the terms of trade deteriorated.

Between 1983 and 1987, the economy failed to grow, with the possible exception of a temporary spurt in 1983–4 associated with favourable weather conditions for food crops and increased mineral exports (Table 4.1). Budgetary performance was also lamentable. While the June 1986 budget, for example, projected revenues (including grants) of Le 1451.7 million and expenditures of Le 1622.5 million, revised estimates in February 1987 projected an overall deficit of Le 1566.3 million – some 800 per cent over estimate. In the meantime, revenues had fallen short by 48 per cent of target while the Leone had depreciated by more than 350 per cent.

Table 4.1. Sierra Leone, GDP, at factor cost by kind of economic activity (at 1984–5 prices, in millions of Leones)

Item	1984–5	1985–6	1986–7
Agriculture, forestry, hunting and fishing	2070.2	1969.4	2120.4
Mining and quarrying	292.1	328.4	343.0
Manufacturing and handicrafts	169.8	162.5	150.4
Electricity and water supply	12.2	10.6	7.6
Construction	127.9	131.8	136.5
Wholesale and retail trade; hotels and restaurants	758.3	762.6	759.2
Transport, storage and communications	545.9	439.7	399.6
Finance, insurance, real estate, and other business services	433.9	436.4	456.6
Other services	102.1	108.9	115.9
Producers of government services	143.0	154.4	177.2
Less imputed service charges and financial intermediaries	35.0	–36.9	–38.3
GDP at factor costs	4620.4	4467.8	4628.1

Source: Central Statistics Office, Freetown, Sierra Leone.

Public spending has come to concentrate on debt service, which accounted for an average of 24.3 per cent of annual expenditures between 1983 and 1990. In comparison, education has received 14.3 per cent, national defence 5.9 per cent, health care 5.5 per cent, and agriculture, 3.8 per cent (Table 4.2). Spending has outstripped revenues in all fiscal years except 1987–8, a major consequence of which has been mounting dependence on the banking system: domestic bank lending to government increased by more than 330 per cent between 1980 and 1985.

External imbalances have complemented these domestic structural imbalances. Current accounts deficits, relatively small and manageable (i.e., less than 5 per cent of GDP) before 1973, rose to 13.3 per cent of GDP in 1982. With the exception of rutile

Table 4.2. Sierra Leone, sectoral expenditures as percentage of total expenditures, 1983–90

Sector	1983–4	1984–5	1985–6	1986–7	1987–8	1988–9[1]	1989–90[2]
General services	16.1	14.3	6.8	28.1	28.4	7.3	11.4
National defence	5.1	5.8	1.9	8.2	9.4	4.1	6.5
Education	19.1	19.1	5.9	18.8	20.6	7.3	9.1
Health	8.8	7.4	2.6	7.4	8.7	2.2	1.3
Agriculture and natural resources	6.9	3.6	1.7	4.1	7.2	1.5	1.9
Unallocable appropriation	0.4	0.7	0.0	1.3	1.7	2.4	5.2
Public debt	22.6	20.0	68.3	0.0	0.2	58.8	52.2

1 Figures for 1988–9 are anticipated actuals.
2 Figures for 1989–90 are estimates.
Source: Sierra Leone Government, *Estimates of Revenue and Expenditure*, Various Years.

and bauxite, exports declined in volume over the period. Agricultural products gained at the expense of the declining minerals sector (Table 4.3). Imports – rice and crude oil above all – have grown faster than exports (Table 4.4).

On the micro-level, per capita income has sharply deteriorated. While the figures show an increase in nominal terms from Le 326.7 to Le 5263.7 between 1980 and 1987, this was largely the consequence of inflation and the devaluation of the Leone. If the trend is deflated using the exchange rate parity in US dollars, per capita income at the end of the period is seen to have been roughly half its initial value. This sharply expresses the decline in the quality of life as a consequence of the social costs of adjustment. Concomitantly, the differential between wage-earning workers in the mainly urban formal sector, on the one hand, and informal-sector workers and subsistence farmers on the other appears to be growing, though overall income distribution has changed little, and still confirms the conclusions of the 1976 JASPA Report on Sierra Leone. It found that incomes were heavily skewed in favour of large-scale entrepreneurs, big retailers, etc., a category accounting for less than 10 per cent of the population but earning more than 30 per cent of national income; that concentration of wealth was increasing; and that government policies to redistribute income or safeguard against further inequalities were almost wholly lacking. (Eliott *et al.*, 1990)

Upward wage adjustments introduced after 1986 have been rendered ineffective by the absence of price controls and the removal of subsidies on rice and petroleum products. Not only have nominal wages failed to keep pace with food, housing, and education costs, but incomes have been further affected by the tax structure. It thus seems that the brunt of the adjustment programme has been borne by the wage-earning poor, especially in the urban areas. At the same time, these 'vulnerable groups' have developed new coping mechanisms in response to the deterioration in their standard of living.

As the economy went into crisis after 1980, the Sierra Leone government maintained an overvalued official exchange rate, resulting in the diversion of foreign

Table 4.3. Sierra Leone, exports of selected commodities, 1983–6 (volume in thousands of metric tons unless otherwise specified; value in millions of Leones)

Item	1983		1984		1985		1986	
	Volume	Value	Volume	Value	Volume	Value	Volume	Value
Agriculture								
Cocoa	12.5	29.1	9.9	58.1	10.2	88.5	8.6	196.7
Coffee	3.1	7.7	2.1	34.3	10.4	160.2	7.4	164.5
Ginger	0.1	0.1	0.1	1.1	–	0.6	–	0.5
Kola nuts	0.9	0.6	0.3	0.3	0.7	0.7	1.2	4.6
Palm kernel	8.4	2.0	13.1	13.0	8.3	11.2	2.0	6.0
Piassava	1.5	0.5	0.5	0.2	1.1	0.7	1.1	2.4
Shrimp	1.3	7.1	0.7	5.0	0.7	9.2	1.3	67.7
Tobacco	–	–	–	–	0.1	2.1	0.3	19.9
Minerals								
Bauxite	523.7	12.6	998.3	47.4	718.8	58.9	1550.6	75.1
Diamonds (m carats)	299.2	60.3	474.6	127.8	220.8	64.7	305.6	122.8
Gold (m grams)	52.2	1.3	82.7	1.8	82.7	3.5	192.6	36.4
Iron ore	67.3	0.1	422.2	10.9	–	–	–	–
Rutile	46.2	20.8	94.7	59.7	77.9	117.6	120.5	342.3
Other		9.1		11.3		26.9		74.2
Totals		151.7		370.9		548.9		1113.2

Source: Central Statistics Office, Freetown, Sierra Leone.

Table 4.4. Sierra Leone, imports by commodity sections, 1983–6 (millions of Leones)

Commodity Section	1983 Value	1983 %	1984 Value	1984 %	1985 Value	1985 %	1986 Value	1986 %
Food, live animals	70.7	25.4	54.4	13.0	237.7	30.2	607.4	26.2
Beverages, tobacco	2.8	1.0	6.8	1.6	15.8	2.0	64.0	2.7
Crude materials (except fuels)	3.8	1.4	4.1	1.0	6.3	0.8	34.8	1.5
Mineral fuels, lubricants, related materials	96.6	34.7	162.7	39.0	168.6	21.6	258.6	11.1
Animal and vegetable oils; fats and waxes	3.1	1.1	4.5	1.1	4.9	0.6	57.9	2.5
Chemicals	15.4	5.5	21.4	5.1	38.1	4.9	203.5	8.8
Manufactured goods, as materials	34.5	12.4	66.6	15.9	1098.8	13.9	366.5	15.8
Machinery, transport equipment	41.5	14.9	80.4	19.3	166.1	21.3	629.5	27.1
Miscellaneous manu-factured goods	8.7	3.2	14.7	3.5	29.9	3.8	84.7	3.7
Miscellaneous	1.0	0.4	1.9	0.5	7.4	0.9	14.3	0.6
Totals	278.1	100.0	417.6	100.0	781.6	100.0	231.3	100.0

Source: Central Statistics Office, Freetown, Sierra Leone.

exchange away from official channels and thereby tightening the squeeze on public-sector spending. Imprudent borrowing in the late 1970s now produced an end-loading problem, with sharply increasing external obligations. Despite periodic relief, the country's debt stood at Le 869.5 million (SDR766 million) by 1984, or about 38 per cent of GDP, while the debt-service ratio had shot up to 300 per cent of total export earnings by the following year. Three devaluations of the Leone in 1983–6 proved ineffectual. In the same period, public expenditures quadrupled in nominal terms, owing largely to poor budgetary control and mismanagement in parastate enterprises. Foreign investor confidence was seriously weakened, and this further eroded domestic confidence as well.

Against this background, the government sought IMF assistance in 1986 and initiated a Medium Term Structural Adjustment Programme aimed at restoring the real growth rate to 3 per cent per annum (just offsetting population growth), reducing inflation from a current 90 per cent to 10 per cent in 1988–9, and cutting the external current account deficit in half, to 1 per cent of GDP by 1988–9. Policy changes called for under the programme included exchange rate adjustments, import liberalization, reduction of the budget deficit, containment of monetary growth, and the correction of domestic price disturbances. This plan was soon expanded into a comprehensive, three-year 'Programme for Rehabilitation and Economic Recovery' under which a structural adjustment loan from the World Bank was secured. The medium-term policy framework called for the following, *inter alia:*

1   stimulating private sector participation in agricultural and industrial production through market incentives and pricing policies;
2   improving the efficiency of public services through greater accountability and better management of available resources;
3   reforming parastate enterprises and reducing their size by half;
4   restructuring and strengthening fiscal and monetary policies;
5   institution-building in agriculture, budget supervision, and investment planning, through civil-service reform and other measures;
6   attaining balance-of-payments stability in the context of a liberal trade and payments system.

The programme envisaged growth coming principally in the agricultural sector, inasmuch as the bulk of the population was concentrated there and the benefits would have an immediate effect. Exports of minerals (gold, rutile, bauxite) were also expected to grow, as were maritime products. But the sanguine projections failed to materialize; the programme was overambitious, and the government's commitment to the reform measures faltered in the face of mounting resistance by entrenched interests. As the economy deteriorated further in 1987, the President declared a State of Economic Emergency and assumed extraordinary powers to combat corruption, smuggling, and hoarding of essential goods and currency. By 1988 the reform programme had been abandoned altogether; currency depreciation and inflationary pressures resumed, and investor confidence dropped further. A new market-oriented programme was adopted in late 1989, featuring a 'managed floating system' of exchange rates jointly administered by the government, the Central Bank, and commercial banks. At this writing, discussions are under way with the IMF and World Bank to work out the details of a new fund-assisted package.

Why the Programme Failed

In accounting for the failure of the structural adjustment programme in Sierra Leone, three facets of such efforts must be examined: theoretical assumptions, administrative weaknesses, and the social costs of adjustment.

A fundamental flaw in such programmes is their built-in tendency toward internally contradictory approaches. The attempt to reduce aggregate demand, a typical feature, induces disincentives to the expansion of supply. Measures aimed at improving resource allocation (raising producer prices, reducing tariffs, etc.) involve a reduction of public revenues, which can be a counter-stabilization force at times of excessive demand pressures. And because structural adjustment financing is usually conditional on short-term policy measures by regimes operating in a framework of openness to the international economy, little room is left for flexibility in the face of exogenous constraints on growth. Thus the timing and phasing of adjustment programmes often decide their success or failure. At the international level, adjustment programmes can fall victim to the 'fallacy of composition'; that is, concentration on price incentives to promote export expansion in a series of countries can result in a glut on the world market and a consequent further worsening of the commodity terms of trade.

On the administrative level, unwarranted presuppositions are made regarding the availability of managerial resources to implement measures such as budgetary controls, fiscal reforms, and reduction of *ad hoc* interventions. There is a further tacit assumption that the government is committed to meeting its part of the social contract. When these assumptions fail to reflect the realities, recourse is made to privatization, often resulting in the replacement of public controls with control by non-indigenous monopolies. The public interest is sacrificed and efficiency fails to materialize.

Finally, the social trade-offs of adjustment programmes need to be taken fully into account, addressing questions such as, What is the magnitude of the social costs owing to curtailment of public spending? To what extent will vulnerable groups be affected? Who will bear the ultimate costs of adjustment? It is also pertinent to examine the implications of a failed adjustment programme, the dangers posed by 'adjustment fatigue', and the attendant psychological costs of resuscitating the process.

It would be rather harsh to blame Sierra Leone's failure simply on mismanagement of the economy. As adjustment began to be implemented, there was an immediate surge of inflation in urban areas and an adverse shift in the commodity terms of trade. In the immediate post-adjustment period (1986–7), the prices of rice, petroleum, kerosene, and urban transport rose by more than 200 per cent, 587 per cent, 1,025 per cent, and 155 per cent respectively. (The rather low increase in urban transport was due to government intervention in holding down fares.) Wages in the formal sector failed to match these price hikes. Real wages declined 26 per cent between 1986 and 1988. In export crops, producer prices were lifted substantially but supply was not sufficiently elastic to overcome the declining trend. Devaluation of the Leone brought increases in input prices (e.g., for fertilizers and seedlings), which served to further depress supply responses.

The Impact of Adjustment

The need for structural adjustment in sub-Saharan Africa is widely accepted. When countries fail to take domestic measures to conform to the exigencies of the international environment and instead pursue policies that promote fiscal and trade imbalances, adjustment becomes a punitive resort. What is questionable is the design of the programmes, the pace and sequencing of reforms, and, particularly, the social costs of structural adjustment, especially for those least able to cope – the marginalized rural and urban poor. The implications have become urgent in the light of various studies indicating that the proportion of the sub-Saharan African population living below the poverty line increased from 30–40 per cent in the mid-1970s to 50–75 per cent in the mid-1980s (Wolfson, 1985).

The pressures exerted through structural adjustment have been particularly severe with respect to spending on social services. This area appears to be particularly vulnerable to reduction in budgetary outlays because it is usually regarded by governments as a 'soft option', and because its notorious inefficiencies prompt the IMF to press for cutbacks. Increasingly, governments have been unable to maintain effective provision of social services such as health care and education. The financial burden is then transferred to the private sector through such schemes as cost recovery in health care and full-cost tuition fees.

In order to evaluate the impact of such policy orientations on the social services sector, it is necessary to examine the efficacy of the adjustment programme in attaining stated national objectives. Performance criteria should be based on a 'four A's' rule: improvements in the service must be *accessible, acceptable, affordable,* and *adaptable.* We shall examine both the pre-adjustment and post-adjustment periods.

Health Care

The major causes of morbidity and mortality in Sierra Leone are malaria, tuberculosis, leprosy, whooping cough, measles, tetanus, and respiratory illnesses. While hospital statistics seriously understate the severity of these problems, they do reflect the patterns of incidence and prevalence. The overall health situation in the country can be seen from these 1989 indices: Crude Death Rate: 24 per 1000; Infant Mortality: 160 per 1000 live births; life expectancy: 40 years (for both sexes).

In 1989, there were 317 medical practitioners (and only 19 dentists) in the country, or roughly one doctor for every 12,000 persons. More than 60 per cent of physicians were employed by the government, although most had private practices as well. The government has supported the training of paramedical and auxiliary personnel to augment staffing at health facilities. The University of Sierra Leone has had a Department of Community Health at Fourah Bay College since 1978, and in 1989 a College of Medicine and Allied Health Services was established to train doctors, dentists and pharmacists.

Of the 58 hospitals existing in 1989, 27 were government-run, 12 were operated by missions, and 19 were private or industrial. There were as well 479 clinics, including 129 Community Health Centres (CHC), 143 Community Health Posts (CHP), 131

Maternal and Child Health Posts (NCHP), and 30 mission clinics. The 4065 hospital beds available in 1987 resulted in a ratio of one bed per 914 persons.

As a signatory of the Alma Ata Declaration, which set the goal of adequate health care for all by the year 2000, Sierra Leone's government outlined a Health Sector Plan for 1983–7. Broad policy objectives included:

1 establishing a network of appropriately staffed and logistically functional health services, comprehensively managed and available to all citizens;
2 strengthening health legislation and services so as to protect citizens from environmental health hazards and communicable disease; and
3 fostering community participation and intersectoral cooperation in accordance with the Primary Health Care (PHC) concept.
   In concretizing these projections, the government has focused on the provision of rural-based medical facilities with the aim of
4 preventing the spread of malaria, tuberculosis, leprosy, measles, and other such ailments by extending Endemic Control Units to the district level;
5 reducing infant mortality by strengthening maternal and child health care;
6 building a network of rural health centres and improving existing units; and
7 increasing the country's training capacity.

These objectives have clearly been exceedingly ambitious, at a time when budgetary constraints have reduced the availability of resources for the health care system. Even before the adjustment programmes were imposed, only 3 per cent of health expenditures in the fiscal years 1981–4 was available for capitalization; wages and salaries accounted for 55 per cent, only about 16 per cent went for drug procurement. The rest was devoted to other recurrent costs, within which the proportion available for medical equipment declined. Of the total state budget during 1983–90, the proportion allocated for health care declined from 8.8 per cent at the outset to a projected 1.3 per cent in 1989–90; an average of 5.8 per cent went for health care over the period (Table 4.2).

Immunization efforts have been conducted since 1982 with the support of UNICEF and the Italian government. This Extended Programme of Immunization (EPI) has aimed principally at protecting infants and pregnant women. However, a base-line survey of the EPI's effectiveness in 1984 revealed that less than 15 per cent of those under five years of age were fully immunized.

Medical personnel have been overly concentrated in the urban areas and especially in Freetown. The latter and its environs (the Western Area) account for 58 per cent of all medical doctors and more than 70 per cent of all dental surgeons. Most of the remainder are located in urban settlements, and scarcely any are to be found in the rural areas. Mobile clinics to serve the countryside are still at a rudimentary level, and poor administration and weak logistical support have constrained their effectiveness.

Inefficiency also pervades the management of drug supplies, and the PHC sector has been largely reliant on pharmaceuticals purchased on the open market. Implementation of a cost-recovery system in 1986 checked the worst excesses, but the programme's effectiveness has been limited owing to the unavailability of many drugs. Prior to the cost-recovery programme, medical services were provided almost free of charge (e.g., prescriptions were priced at 40 cents per patient). But unit prices of drugs have escalated sharply since 1987, resulting in a general loss of confidence in the PHC system. Since then, rural communities have increasingly resorted to traditional sources of medical care, a trend also observed for the urban poor. As to future drug supplies, ministry officials are optimistic and cite the government's recourse to UNICEF's Drug Procurement Facility as a means of reducing reliance on drugs supplied by private (domestic and foreign) contractors.

Most indicators point to a deterioration of health systems. Providing adequate health services while carrying out economic adjustment presents a major dilemma. Improved efficacy of the cost-recovery programme could generate more income to devote to health expenditures. Administrative reorganization could augment the autonomy of local authorities and in turn serve as a basis for improving accountability. Procuring drugs at world-market prices will contribute to cost effectiveness, but UNICEF's Drug Procurement Facility must be more intensively utilized to reduce the burden on vulnerable groups. At present the lack of a universal health insurance programme effectively precludes formal medical treatment for a large proportion of the population. To cushion the effects of deteriorating living conditions due to structural adjustment, it is necessary to design rudimentary schemes to tackle these problems. For instance, a nominal premium could be charged for school-going children to enable them to be properly treated.

Efficiency of health-care delivery has been enhanced by the implementation of the PHC system, but there is still much room for improvement. Reliance has been placed much more on static units (hospitals, health centres) than on mobile clinics, but transport difficulties and commuting distances place tremendous strains on rural communities. Increasing the outreach of mobile clinics could provide wider coverage in the countryside as well as servicing the deprived areas in peri-urban zones.

As to acceptability, there is need for closer integration of 'traditional' and 'modern' modes of health care. Research into herbal and other forms of treatment is urgently required; one advantage could be the scaling back of drug imports to the country. The performance of Traditional Birth Attendants (TBA) has been impressive; steps are needed to improve their service conditions and integrate them further into the care provided by the Ministry. The role of village health workers must be reinforced and fully incorporated into the PHC system, and greater stress must be placed on community participation.

Education

According to Sierra Leone's 1985 Census, only about 40 per cent of children between the ages of five and twelve were enrolled in primary schools. The rapidly growing population and its relative youthfulness (median age, 19 years) imply that resource demands for education are mounting exponentially while GDP stagnates in real terms.

Government objectives with regard to education have evolved since independence. Programmes such as the Development Programme in Education (1964–70) and the White Paper on Education Policy (1970) sought to implement the ideals established at the UNESCO Conference of African Ministers of Education, held in Addis Ababa in 1961: that free compulsory primary education should be provided by 1980, and that 30 per cent of all primary school leavers should complete secondary school (UNESCO, 1961). The 1979 Educational Sector Review recommended the following steps:

1   a nationwide primary school construction programme;
2   a set of measures to enhance internal efficiency of the education delivery system;
3   primary teacher training; and
4   production of textbooks and ancillary materials, especially at the primary level.

Low levels of literacy have been recognized as a central problem. Estimates put illiteracy in the country as a whole at 85 per cent, but rates in the rural areas are as high as 98 per cent. Improving rural communities' access to education was the objective of the Bunumbu Project, initiated in 1973 under the auspices of the United Nations Development Programme.

For the period 1965–86, educational expenditures averaged 20.5 per cent of the overall government budget. Allocations to primary schooling have accounted for the largest single category of the education budget, averaging 39.8 per cent during the 1980s (Table 4.5). Secondary education, the next-largest category, accounted for an average of 29.6 per cent. Subsidies and subventions – grants to the University and to teachers colleges, contributions to UNESCO and other bodies, etc. – rank third. Within the latter rubric, the University receives 60 per cent of all expenditures and teachers colleges get 31 per cent, on average. Sharp declines set in in the 1985 fiscal year, however, and since 1987 the percentage devoted to education has fallen by more than 50 per cent. Funds allocated to the Ministry of Education amounted to less than 2.8 per cent of the budget for the 1989–90 fiscal year.

The effects of adjustment are seen most dramatically in the evolution of unit costs with respect to enrolment (Table 4.6). When inflation and currency devaluation are taken into account, spending per enrolled student is seen to have fallen drastically in the 1980s: by 84 per cent at the primary and secondary levels, and by nearly 90 per cent in technical training.

And the level of unsatisfied needs for education continues to grow. Given the trend in real unit costs, the government's current expenditures for primary schooling must increase at better than 6.5 per cent per annum merely to offset the effects of inflation, and by a further 2.5 per cent per annum to meet expected yearly increases in enrolment. This means spending on primary schooling must rise by 9 per cent annually, not including replacement costs of capital, which are intensified through accelerated depreciation of buildings and equipment. A similar pattern obtains at the secondary level, where enrolment is projected to rise 2.8 per cent per annum and where the trend in real unit costs dictates a further rise of 6 per cent per annum, for a total growth rate of 8.8 per cent. Controlling for capital depreciation, real growth in this area should be at least 10 per cent annually. Vocational-technical training has grown at an average of 5 per cent per annum, while unit costs in real terms have been falling. This is at odds with the government's own policy objectives. Finally, even to restore the levels of 1975–6 for these three areas, the government's current expenditures must increase by more than 420 per cent. This is obviously not feasible in the present circumstances.

Table 4.5. Sierra Leone, educational expenditures by subsector, 1980–6, as percentage of total spending

Subsector	1980–1	1981–2	1982–3	1983–4	1984–5	1985–6
Primary education	41.2	38.1	38.7	39.8	40.4	40.7
Secondary education	27.9	28.1	31.2	29.7	29.9	30.5
Teacher education	0.1	0.1	0.0	0.0	0.0	0.1
Technical education	2.0	2.1	1.9	1.7	1.7	2.3
Teaching aids	0.3	0.2	0.0	0.2	0.1	0.2
Subsidies/subventions	17.8	21.0	18.9	17.2	14.3	16.4
Planning unit	0.2	0.2	0.1	0.1	0.0	0.2
Administration	10.5	10.0	8.9	11.1	10.4	9.7

Source: Government Estimates of Revenue and Expenditures; author's estimates (1985–6).

Table 4.6. Sierra Leone, education expenditures in relation to enrolment, 1980–6

	1980–1	1981–2	1982–3	1983–4	1984–5	1985–6
Primary level						
Recurrent expenditures (mill. Le)	19.27	19.95	21.77	28.68	31.35	36.76
Total student enrolment (000s)	263.72	276.91	290.76	294.83	292.21	389.94
Unit cost, current prices	73.0	69.0	74.9	98.4	107.3	94.3
Unit cost, constant 1980 prices	73.0	56.7	46.3	35.9	22.6	11.7
Secondary level						
Recurrent expenditures (mill. Le)	13.05	14.72	17.55	21.42	23.23	27.57
Total student enrolment (000s)	63.30	66.46	69.79	69.98	70.18	98.00
Unit cost, current prices	206.2	221.5	179.9	306.0	331.0	281.4
Unit cost, constant 1980 prices	206.2	179.6	111.3	111.6	69.8	34.9
Technical/vocational						
Recurrent expenditures (mill. Le)	0.92	1.09	1.06	1.26	1.30	2.05
Total student enrolment (000s)	0.95	0.95	0.97	0.97	0.98	3.02
Unit cost, current prices	970.5	1146.6	1098.9	1293.5	1324.0	679.6
Unit cost, constant 1980 prices	970.5	929.9	680.0	471.7	279.4	84.3

Source: Ministry of Development and Economic Planning; author's estimates (1985–87).

In the light of this constraint, it is imperative to examine more closely the effectiveness of government spending on education.

Three types of primary schools are recognized – assisted, independent, and private – and in addition there are a plethora of unrecognized units known as 'feeder' schools, each anchored to a 'parent' school. While this arrangement can perhaps be justified for kindergarten pupils, there is evidence it has been grossly abused by school proprietors: the government has an open-ended commitment to provide funds for salaries, other personnel emoluments, and equipment grants for such 'unplanned' schools; they represent some 21 per cent of the total school population. About 9 per cent of primary schools are government-assisted, with grants provided to meet teachers' salaries, books, and other sundry operating costs. Independent schools are those owned and run outside the direct control of the Ministry of Education but required to meet minimum standards. Private schools receive no government grants but still account for a significant proportion of enrolment; they are mostly sub-standard in quality.

Since the primary schools depend almost exclusively on government support, the stabilization measures adopted after 1986 have considerably curtailed the resources available to this sector. The government provides a grant of 4 Leone per pupil per annum, largely inadequate even before the drastic decline in the Leone's purchasing power. Essential materials – textbooks, visual aids, chalk boards, furniture, potable water, and toilets – are either in short supply or absent altogether, especially in rural schools. In view of chronically high drop-out and repeater rates, education at this level was reorganized in 1984. Duration of the programme was reduced from seven years to six, and the entry age was increased from five years of age to six. The aim was to reduce expenditure on primary education while ensuring greater efficiency, but there has been no evaluation to date of the impact of these changes.

Secondary schooling in Sierra Leone is largely grammar-school oriented, reflecting colonial patterns. Earlier attempts to diversify the curriculum and include vocational and technical training, and agricultural theory and practice, proved inadequate in shifting the orientation away from its original pattern. Successful candidates in the O-level examinations (i.e., those with five or more subjects) can be admitted directly to the University at the preliminary-year level; others follow a further two-year programme and, upon passing the A-level examination, can be admitted to the University at the intermediate-year level. A recent educational census reported 213 secondary schools in the country; the number enrolled increased by about 2.8 per cent annually from 1975 to 1986. But the drop-out rate at the entry level is estimated at 34 per cent. When one adds the drop-out rate in subsequent years (37–40 per cent), the cumulative result shows only about 27 per cent of those entering Form I having any measure of success. The economy's inability to absorb these school-leavers condemns most to unemployment.

Technical and vocational training institutes increased from four in 1975 to eighteen in 1988 (UNICEF, 1989). But enrolment at these institutes has remained low, growing only from 840 to 3015 in 1985. While no comprehensive studies have been done on those graduating from such schools, the ILO/JASPA study on Sierra Leone suggests the dominance of informal sector activities (ILO/JASPA, 1978, 1984). In Freetown, less than 14 per cent of entrepreneurs surveyed had any formal training or, for that matter, functional literacy. This points up the inadequacy of the technical-vocational institutes in meeting mid-level personnel needs. The major reasons for this deficiency rest on a shortage of qualified staff, physical facilities, equipment, and materials.

Enrolment for all teachers colleges rose from 1848 to 3304 for the 1985–6 academic year. Success rates remained low, averaging only about 33 per cent of total enrolment. Moreover, the rate has been falling since 1981. A by-product of the deepening recession has been a slowing of demand for teachers, and teacher morale has been weakened as well by irregular payment of salaries.

At the apex of formal education in the country is the University of Sierra Leone, comprised of Fourah Bay College, Njala University College, the College of Medical and Allied Sciences, and various Institutes. Enrolment at this level showed a modest increase from 1705 in 1978–9 to 2314 in 1985–6. The teaching staff grew more rapidly, from 240 to 324 for the same period, and scope remains for expanding the student population. The latter entails expansion of the physical facilities, however, and this appears to be the most pressing constraint.

Non-formal education in Sierra Leone is offered by a host of agencies. In 1967, the Ministry of Education assumed overall responsibility for both adult literacy and adult education. A National Literacy Committee was set up and empowered to coordinate, supervise, and provide policy input for literacy programmes. A 1980 report estimated that, among adults 15 years and over, where illiteracy was as high as 80.5 per cent, only 7865 persons were enrolled in any literacy programme (Gupta, 1980). A recent national directory gives the number of adult education providers as 114, even smaller than Gupta's 1980 estimate of 123. There has been no recent evaluation of the operation of the adult literacy programme; all indicators show that the programme's influence has been marginal and that there is considerable scope for improving the coverage and intensity of the effort.

This descriptive analysis provides a background for examining the educational situation and shows the long-standing inadequacies and inefficiency in its delivery systems. Stabilization measures have had a further devastating effect on educational services. In examining the implications, we focus on three areas: school clustering and deployment; educational costs borne by parents; and the role of the Ministry in resource management, distribution, and monitoring.

The teacher/pupil ratio at the primary level is about 1 : 32, but the ratio for qualified teachers is more like 1 : 82. This shows the paucity of trained teachers at this level and underscores the importance of increased training. Enrolment ratios show wide regional variations. The Western area records the highest rate, 81 per cent; the Northern province the lowest, 26 per cent; and the Southern and Eastern provinces record rates of 42 per cent each. There is as well a marked disparity between the urban and rural areas, with the former averaging 75 per cent as compared to 20 per cent in the latter. The clustering pattern is similar at the secondary level but the concentration around Freetown is still more pronounced.

Austerity measures have brought further concentration. Increased migration from the rural to urban areas and to Freetown in particular has led to a desertion of the provincial towns by qualified teachers. Nonetheless, the government has stated that its main priority is to improve access to education in the rural areas. Realization of this objective should involve differential inducements to qualified teachers willing to reside in rural locations.

Education is a quasi-public good. To the extent that it provides benefits to society at large rather than to the recipient alone, there is justification for public subsidies to education. But education also enables the recipient to earn a better living and thus constitutes an investment; hence user costs ought to be borne to an extent by parents and guardians. The problem is one of striking a balance: which costs are to be borne by government, and which are to be borne privately? (Mongat and Tan, 1986).

While tuition fees at the primary and secondary levels have been abolished in Sierra Leone, this has been offset by increasing 'hidden' costs borne by parents and guardians for textbooks, stationery, uniforms, travel, and extra tuition for night classes. Total and individual resource costs of education in Sierra Leone have not been computed on a comprehensive basis, but a sample survey conducted in 1989 yielded cost internalization coefficients of 0.35, 0.59, and 0.28 for primary, secondary, and university education respectively. Thus the main burdens on parents and guardians come at the secondary level. (At the university level such costs are much reduced owing to the prevalence of scholarships and other grants-in-aid.) It would thus appear that the stabilization measures have been particularly hard on those with children in secondary school. Government action has focused mainly on standardizing textbooks in line with curricula developed by the Institute of Education and on making these books available at affordable prices. Textbook revenues are expected to yield a revolving fund to ensure the sustainability of the programme after the initial three years. No details of the programme's performance have yet been made public. But such provision is highly desirable in that it would eliminate the oligopolies long enjoyed by street vendors of second-hand textbooks.

The Ministry of Education, Cultural Affairs, and Sports is directly responsible for all decisions regarding education in the country. The system is highly centralized in Freetown, although Regional Principal Education Officers have been appointed for the three provinces. It is evident that the Ministry's operations are inefficient in terms of monitoring resource disbursements. Budget estimates for 1986–7, for example, called for Le 27 million in teacher salaries, but this was totally exhausted in the second quarter; actual salary expenditures for the fiscal year totalled Le 54 million, or exactly twice the estimate. The widespread existence of feeder schools, outside the Ministry's control but reliant on it for financial support, serves to compound the problem of monitoring.

Staff morale in the schools is low owing to the Ministry's perceived inefficiency and especially to the wage structure for teachers. Real wages for both untrained and trained teachers have declined by more than 74 per cent since 1980. When this is coupled with the long delays encountered in payment of salaries, the root cause of high teacher turnover rates, especially in the primary schools, is evident.

To summarize: while there have been nominal increases in government expenditures on education, resource allocation in real terms has been declining. Moreover, the bulk of resources has been directed into recurrent expenditures, especially salaries and other personnel emoluments. But educational resource demands continue to grow, and projections into the mid-1990s indicate that expenditures must increase fourfold merely to maintain current levels of enrolment, teacher/pupil ratio, grants-in-aid, and so on. Inasmuch as this is hardly feasible given other competing demands on government, it becomes imperative to consider the scope for educational reforms that would enable government to attain its stated objectives.

Policy has been oriented towards 'basic' education: stressing primary and secondary schooling, ruralization, technical-vocational training, and adult literacy. As for the University, policy has been directed toward a more functional approach stressing income-generating activities. Expenditure patterns, however, do not appear to conform to the stated goals. Relatively speaking, the primary schools have suffered most and the pattern of clustering tends to favour disproportionately the urban as opposed to the rural areas. Success rates have been low and show no trend toward improvement. The mushrooming of substandard feeder schools that rely on the Ministry for sustenance but are not accountable to it has led government into an impasse of open-ended commitments. And marked weaknesses in financial management have created scope for malpractice.

Finally, the wage structure has failed to provide the necessary inducements. The deterioration of morale, especially among teachers, highlights their increasing inability to earn a living wage. In a circular fashion, this further weakens internal efficiency.

Employment

Empirical evidence on employment in Sierra Leone is unreliable and scanty. The working population was estimated at 908,147 persons by the 1963 Census. By 1974 this had increased by about 11 per cent to 1,009,872. Of that number, 46 per cent were self-employed, unpaid household workers accounted for 36 per cent, and employers made up but 0.3 per cent. The high percentage of self-employed was highlighted by the Second Draft National Development Plan for 1981–6, which concluded that inasmuch as the formal sector of the economy could not possibly absorb all those needing jobs, emphasis had to be put on the promotion of development largely through 'aided self-help' schemes.

The public sector accounted for 65 per cent of those working for wages, according to the 1974 Census. A considerable sex differential was evident, with females making up only 28 per cent of the total labour force and accounting for less than 12 per cent of public-sector workers.

At present detailed results from the 1985 Census have yet to be published. Some inferences can be drawn from research findings of a *Pilot Survey on the Labour Force*, conducted by the Central Statistics Office (1988) and from average yearly employment statistics from the same office. Table 4.7 gives a breakdown of average yearly waged employment for establishments having six or more workers. This does not include subsistence agriculture or informal sector activities. This subsector rose from 67,750 in 1983 to a peak of 73,712 in 1986, then shrank markedly in 1987 to 59,089 as a consequence of stabilization measures. Government services showed a slight increase, however, owing to resistance to streamlining and reorganizing the public sector. Construction and mining/quarrying declined throughout the period. The former reflected the deepening recession and the subsequent increases in the prices of building materials. As noted above, mining activities declined owing to the depletion of alluvial deposits in the diamond mining areas.

It is instructive to look at labour participation rates, dependency ratios, and unemployment rates, as shown in Table 4.8. The figures reveal that, in 1988, the labour participation rate (i.e., the ratio of the number of persons in active employment to the size of the employable population) was higher in the rural areas as compared to urban ones. The rate was also much higher for men than for women. The dependency ratio (i.e., the proportion of the number of persons not working to those productively

Table 4.7. Sierra Leone, average yearly employment in establishments with six or more workers, by industry group, 1983–7

Industry group	Total employed					As % of sector's labour force				
	1983	1984	1985	1986	1987	1983	1984	1985	1986	1987
Agriculture, forestry, fishing	5812	5833	5951	7051	7090	8.6	8.5	8.6	8.9	10.2
Mining, quarrying	6087	6226	6348	6357	6896	9.0	9.1	9.1	8.6	10.0
Manufacturing	7943	8071	8142	8341	7474	11.7	11.6	11.7	11.3	10.8
Construction	8248	8986	9117	9181	7289	12.2	13.1	13.1	12.4	10.6
Electricity, water services	2128	2134	2166	2182	2188	3.1	3.1	3.1	3.0	3.2
Commerce	5951	6249	6281	6922	4965	8.8	9.1	9.1	9.5	7.2
Wholesale trade	2254	2592	2871	2985	2541	3.3	3.8	4.1	4.1	3.7
Retail trade	1516	1590	1145	1700	670	2.2	2.3	1.7	2.3	1.0
Banks, insurance	2181	2067	2265	2297	1754	3.2	3.2	3.3	3.1	2.5
Transport, storage, communications	7469	7230	7474	8019	7545	11.0	10.6	10.8	10.9	10.9
Services					25,650					37.1
Government services	6466	6478	6509	7455	7455	11.0	10.6	10.8	10.9	10.9
Educational services	6433	6380	6400	6580	6585	9.5	9.3	9.2	8.9	9.5
Medical, other health services	3670	3681	3690	3791	3800	5.4	5.4	5.3	5.1	5.5
Research, scientific institutions	284	285	286	300	310	0.4	0.4	0.4	0.4	0.4
Other services	7259	6993	7046	7500	7500	10.7	10.2	10.2	10.2	10.9

Source: Ministry of Labour, New England, Freetown.

engaged) averaged about 1.9 for urban areas as compared to 1.1 for rural areas. The urban unemployment rate averaged about 14.8 per cent of the total labour force, which in the rural areas was negligible.

Sierra Leone clearly conforms to the pattern of a ruralized society, despite the growing importance of urbanization. This implies that incomes derived from agricultural activities tend to outstrip those from non-agricultural ones. Secondly, government intervention in terms of incomes and prices usually acts in support of urban workers, resulting in distortions in the domestic commodity terms of trade and tending to worsen urban–rural income differentials. Rural–urban migration intensifies the problem posed by urban unemployment and simultaneously reduces the level of food production.

If one makes projections up to 1999, assuming that labour force participation rates remain at their current levels and that fertility remains at 6.5, the labour force will grow from an estimated 1.4 million to 1.6 million. To match the increase of new entrants into the labour force, at least 19,000 jobs have to be created annually, increasing to about 41,000 by 1999. In an economy where there is already high unemployment and still higher underemployment, unless GDP rises by over 3 per cent per annum in real terms these trends will increase exponentially.

Conclusions

The descriptive analyses in this chapter point up the following with respect to Sierra Leone's experience with structural adjustment:

1 The growing impact of demographic pressures, which have seriously undermined the country's ability to cope with declining levels of productivity;
2 excessive financial indiscipline, with increasing resort to deficit financing;
3 little attempt at structural transformations of the economy; and
4 virtually no growth in the economy since 1980.

The discussion recognizes the dimensions of the problems posed by the imbalance of population growth and the inability of food production to meet the resource demands of the growing population, especially the rapid expansion of the capital city since 1975. Migratory pressures caused by urban-oriented policies and the push factor of declining rural conditions have contributed to worsening the situation.

At the government level, policy responses have been weak and have largely involved a 'knee-jerk' approach to crisis management. The comprehensiveness and sustained input necessary to attaining the desired results have been lacking. A policy framework should evolve wherein budgetary controls could be tightened while being calibrated to cushion the impact on targeted vulnerable groups. The pervasive recourse to extra-budgetary spending should be severely restricted. Urgent steps must be taken to ensure monitoring and evaluation of the delivery systems of public services.

The Sierra Leone economy still exhibits a structural configuration that fails to take into account the changing external environment and the need for self-sustained growth from domestic mobilization of resources. Rapid steps are needed to diversify and

Table 4.8.   Sierra Leone, labour force participation rates, dependency ratios, and unemployment
rates, 1988

Item	Urban			Rural			Total		
	Male	Female	Total	Male	Female	Total	Male	Female	Total
Participation	56.7	48.8	52.7	82.7	60.8	71.7	74.9	57.0	66.1
Dependency ratio			1.9			1.1			1.3
Unemployment	·11.8	18.6	14.8	0.8	2.3	1.5	3.3	6.5	4.7

Source: Central Statistics Office, Pilot Survey of Labour Force (1989).

broaden the export base away from excessive concentration on 'traditional' products.
Market research and information systems need to be developed to take advantage of
other export potentials – maritime products, tropical fruits, other minerals, etc.
Institutional reforms such as those laid down in the African Alternative Framework to
Structural Adjustment Programmes (AAF–SAP) (UNECA, 1989) are needed to
broaden intra-regional trade and hence reduce the dependency syndrome.

The detailed analyses of structural adjustment's impact on health, education, and
employment highlight the gap between the resource demands of these sectors and the
country's weak economic performance. In all three, one observes that it would not be
feasible to expand allocations to meet the growing demands. What can be advanced is
the need for restructuring policies to ensure that these essential services are not impaired
even further. The erosion of real income due to inflation and currency depreciation
makes the need for improved cost-effectiveness even more urgent.

Finally, the socio-political milieu must come to reflect a more growth-oriented
outlook. Human resource development and increasing levels of participatory decision-
making are necessary catalysts for providing equitable growth. While privatization
cannot serve as a panacea, government's role should largely be confined to that of an
umpire to ensure that the public interest is enhanced.

References

J. W. Eliott *et al.* (1990). *Income Distribution, Poverty and the Rural–Urban Gap in Sierra Leone.* Geneva: ILO/JASPA.

H. Gupta (1980). *Report on Adult Literacy.*

ILO/JASPA (1978, 1984). *Ensuring Equity and Growth in Sierra Leone.* Addis Ababa.

A. Mongat and J. P. Tan (1986). 'Expanding Education through User Charges; What Can be Achieved in Malawi and Other LDCs'. *Economics of Education Review,* 5: 273–86.

D. Taylor (1988). 'Varieties of Stabilisation Experience'. Alfred Marshall Lectures, Cambridge University.

UNECA (n.d.). *African Alternative Framework to Structural Adjustment for Socio-Economic Recovery and Transformation.* E/ECA/CM/15/6/Rev 3.

UNESCO (1961). *Report on African Ministers of Education.* Addis Ababa.

UNICEF (1989). *Stabilisation, Structural Adjustment, and Vulnerable Groups in Sierra Leone.*

M. Wolfson (1985). 'Populations in Sub-Saharan Africa'. In T. Rose, ed., *Crisis and Recovery in Sub-Saharan Africa.* Paris: OECD.

5 Senegal

Karamoko Kane

Introduction

Like most African countries, Senegal was able to adjust to a less favourable economic environment during the 1970s by borrowing heavily from foreign lenders. Despite a quadrupling of oil prices, a cycle of droughts, and a decline in per capita GDP over the decade, public and private consumption increased. This led to a situation in which external debt service in 1981 was equal to 40 per cent of the value of the country's exports. The 1980s thus became in Senegal a decade of recovery plans and structural adjustment, leading to a deterioration in living conditions as the population was called upon to reduce spending and become less reliant on state subsidies.

Senegal had a population of about 7 million in 1988, and is projected to have 10 million inhabitants by the year 2000. The average rate of population increase, among the world's highest, was 3 per cent in 1980–8 and has been projected at 3.2 per cent for 1988–2000. The population is relatively young: in 1988 persons under 15 years of age accounted for 46.8 per cent of the overall total.

Structural Adjustment Programmes

The IMF and the balance of payments deficit

From 1978, the structural imbalances noted above began to be unbearable. Thus the authorities adopted in November 1979 a medium-term recovery plan and applied to the International Monetary Fund for assistance. An initial 'extended facility' agreement totalling 184.8 million SDR was concluded in August 1980 and was to cover the 1980–3 period. But implementation was soon interrupted, in November 1980, when payments were suspended owing to Senegal's failure to meet the IMF's macro-economic criteria. Subsequent relations between Senegal and the IMF were marked by

* Translated from the French original text.

a series of breaks and renegotiations. The latest agreement as of this writing was a structural adjustment facility for 400 million SDR in the 1986–9 period (IMF, 1987).

The IMF agreements aimed at short-term reductions in the balance of payments deficit. According to the IMF's analysis, Senegal's problems in this regard were characterized by a surplus in final demand (i.e., public consumption, private consumption, and investment) over GDP. This problem – chronic since the country's independence in 1960 (Table 5.1) – had been facilitated by irrational management practices such as expansionary wage policies, sustained increases in employment and salaries in the public sector, and artificial limits on price rises by means of increasing subsidies. The consequent budget deficits led to a mounting public debt and an overall expansion of credit. The measures mandated by the IMF, it was hoped, would restore a propensity to positive savings and thus enable the Senegalese economy to finance a growing part of its investments from domestic financing.

Table 5.1. Senegal, surplus of final demand over GDP, as percentage of GDP

	1960	1965	1970	1975	1980
GDP	100.0	100.0	100.0	100.0	100.0
Private consumption	67.1	74.8	74.0	72.3	78.1
Public consumption	17.1	74.4	14.9	15.2	22.4
Investment	15.7	11.9	15.7	17.8	15.6
Surplus of resources over jobs	–0.1	–4.1	–4.6	–5.3	–16.1

Source: Calculated from World Bank, Memorandum on the Economy of Senegal (Washington, 1984).

To reduce the budget deficit, the IMF called for specific steps, including:

- increasing the price of basic commodities such as rice, sugar, cooking oil, petroleum products, flour, electricity, and public transport;
- increasing the withholding tax on groundnut producers;
- increasing excise tax rates;
- imposition of a 'solidarity tax';
- freezing wages in the public sector and contracting public expenditures on capital goods;
- limiting employment increases in the public sector; and
- limiting the growth of the money supply and credit.

The World Bank and structural adjustment

Alongside the IMF-promoted measures, Senegal accepted a structural adjustment loan from the World Bank. The latter's analysis of the country's problems focused on structural causes of long-term low growth in GDP. These included:

- misallocation of resources, to the detriment of the agricultural sector and other sectors likely to generate exports;
- a hypertrophied and inefficient public sector; and

- inappropriate price and incentive policies, giving rise to price distortions, wage rigidities, and unwarranted subsidization of consumer goods.

On the macro-economic front, the World Bank's objectives for Senegal dovetailed with the prescriptions of the IMF and included the following:

- determination and realization of an investment floor and minimum financing threshold on net public savings (hence reinforcing the need to reduce the budget deficit);
- reduction of price distortions;
- rationalization of management in the public sector; and
- reform of rural development agencies.

The reorganization programme adopted under the World Bank's structural adjustment loan produced few positive results, as compared to the ambitious objectives. A revised scenario was promulgated in December 1984 and set guidelines for the 1985–92 period. This programme stressed the need to boost growth so that Senegal might reduce its deficits and assure external debt service without undergoing a deflationary process that would further impoverish the population. It called for more sustained structural reforms, as follows:

- transformation of rural institutions, with producers to take on greater responsibility while the state would put at their disposal appropriate services such as marketing and credits;
- long-term improvement in the prospects for creating non-agricultural jobs, through state disengagement from all activities that are more suitable to the private sector;
- lowering of excessive levels of protectionism, which had reduced the efficiency and potential of Senegalese industries; and
- definition of a population and education strategy adapted to the needs of the country's economy.

Social and Economic Consequences of Structural Adjustment

Any analysis of the social and economic consequences of structural adjustment must take into account the impact of the disengagement of the state. To foster long-term economic growth, it became necessary to contract and reorient public expenditure. Reduction of demand compelled the authorities to arbitrate among sectors and areas of expenditure. Thus social sectors were more likely to be affected than those that were more sensitive politically, such as defence. While available statistical data are somewhat scarce and the period covered too short to discern a definite trend, we can still examine the degree of vulnerability of social spending to structural adjustment.

Health care
Despite the unfavourable evolution of GDP per capita, marked progress in social terms

was registered in Senegal in the decades after independence. The gross death rate declined from 23 per 1000 inhabitants in 1965 to 20 per 1000 in 1980, and then dropped further to 18 per 1000 in 1987. Infant mortality declined from 171 per 1000 live births in 1965 to 147 in 1980 and 131 in 1987. It is evident, then, that Senegal has been able to maintain a relatively high level of protection of infants against the principal childhood diseases, in comparison to the rest of sub-Saharan Africa. In 1986–7, for example, 92 per cent of infants were immunized against tuberculosis, the third-highest immunization rate among 45 African countries (World Bank, 1989). Medical personnel ratios improved from one doctor per 19,490 inhabitants and one nurse per 2440 inhabitants in 1965, to one doctor per 13,060 and one nurse per 2030 in 1984. No improvement occurred in nutritional terms, however, with the average daily calorific intake dropping slightly from 2479 in 1965 to 2350 in 1986.

Education

Percentages of age group enrolled improved at all levels of Senegalese education between 1965 and 1987 (World Bank, 1990). Whereas 40 per cent of boys and 29 per cent of girls of primary-school age were enrolled in 1965, 60 per cent of boys and 49 per cent of girls were enrolled in 1987. The respective figures for secondary schooling were 7 per cent boys and 4 per cent girls in 1965 and 15 per cent boys and 10 per cent girls in 1987. Enrolment in higher education, though quite modest, nonetheless tripled from 1 per cent of age group in 1965 to 3 per cent of age group in 1987. The overall rate of primary schooling in Senegal in 1987 was 50 per cent, as compared to rates of, e.g., 27 per cent in Burkina Faso, 18 per cent in Mali, 57 per cent in Morocco, and 95 per cent in Tunisia.

Such progress in health and education is essentially due to the efforts of the state. Reductions in public expenditures will almost automatically affect the state's social action in these fields. To gauge these consequences, we can examine more closely the evolution of the state's operating budget under structural adjustment. Table 5.2 indicates that while health and education accounted for 22.66 per cent of operating expenditures in 1984–5, the proportion allocated to these sectors increased to 27.5 per cent in 1988–9. Following the model proposed by Hicks and Kubisch, we can construct

Table 5.2. Senegal, current budgetary expenditures, 1984–9 (in millions of CFA francs)

	1984–5	1985–6	1986–7	1987–8	1988–9
Education	32.7	34.7	47.1	48.0	51.6
Public health	9.6	10.2	10.7	11.0	10.9
Armed forces	28.1	28.4	28.6	29.0	30.3
Interior	19.7	12.3	20.3	21.5	20.0
Foreign affairs	10.5	11.2	11.9	12.3	12.9
Economy and finance	9.5	10.0	10.7	10.8	11.4
Current budgetary expenditure	186.4	199.2	206.2	216.5	226.8

Source: Bulletin of Black Africa, No. 1424, 6 October 1988.

'vulnerability coefficients' to measure the relative evolution of spending by sector (Hicks and Kubisch, n. d.). If 'e(j)' is the rate of growth of expenditure in sector 'j' and 'E' is the rate of growth of total spending, then the vulnerability coefficient of sector 'j', or 'V(j)', can be calculated as follows:

$$V(j) = \frac{e(j)}{E}$$

If V(j) is negative, sectoral expenditures have evolved in the reverse direction of total spending, and if its absolute value is high in relative terms, the sector will have been sacrificed to the others – in other words, the sector was vulnerable and received lower priority from the authorities. Table 5.3 suggests, then, that even under structural adjustment, education remained an absolute priority for the Senegalese government while health spending bore the brunt of expenditure cutbacks.

Table 5.3.   Senegal, evolution of current public expenditures (Hicks–Kubisch vulnerability coefficients)

Fiscal year	Education	Health	Interior	Foreign affairs	Economy/ finances	Armed forces
1987–8	+7.36	–1.47	–7.08	+4.75	+4.76	+4.58
1988–9	+1.55	–0.31	–1.49	+1.00	+1.00	+0.96

Source: Calculated from data in Bulletin d'Afrique Noire, No. 1424, 6 October 1988.

Agriculture

The logic of structural adjustment runs directly counter to long-standing state policies with regard to agriculture, which since independence has been the predominant sector of the Senegalese economy. More than 70 per cent of the population is engaged in agriculture. Between 1976 and 1980 (the year when structural adjustment began) the share of GDP represented by agriculture went down from 18 per cent to 9.5 per cent and value-added per capita in the rural sector declined by 32.5 per cent. Degradation of rural incomes was curbed, however, through state intervention in accordance with an aid and distribution logic. Structural adjustment has brought a reversal of these policies, with the state gradually disengaging from the rural areas under a New Agricultural Policy that fosters the introduction of the logic of market forces in Senegalese agriculture.

Until the 1980s, state intervention was expanding in rural Senegal, through such programmes as the Agency for Agricultural Marketing (OCA), which was granted a monopoly on the marketing of groundnuts, and the establishment of Regional Centres of Development Assistance (CRAD), which were given the task of fostering modernization throughout the countryside (the OCA and CRAD were consolidated into the National Agency for Cooperation and Development Assistance in 1969). Following a series of unfavourable events in the 1970s – droughts, famines, and the removal of French supports for the export price of groundnuts – oil-processing factories were brought under state control and state intervention was extended to other areas of production through subsidized distribution of fertilizers, equipment, and certain seeds. By the end of the 1970s, rural areas as a whole were rigidly supervised by public or parastatal agencies. Rural development thus conceived proved a failure, however, in financial, technical, and organizational terms.

Financially, chronic and growing budget deficits were registered by the gamut of agencies involved in agriculture. Weak management, misappropriations, and unorthodox staffing policies soon converted these agencies from instances of support for rural development into a sinkhole for billions of francs. In technical terms, the exorbitant sums spent by the state failed altogether to boost agricultural efficiency. Indeed, productivity and farm incomes in the groundnut sector experienced nearly constant decline, while the costs of rice production came nearly to double the world price of rice. And organizationally, state intervention fostered a mentality among farmers such that they came to expect that the public authorities would cancel all their debts and go on providing seeds and fertilizers at subsidized prices. The cooperatives were quickly conquered by local notables and Marabouts and could never operate democratically. After 25 years the state had failed to inculcate economic calculation into the behaviour of farmers.

Under the structural adjustment programmes, state disengagement from agriculture came to be considered a panacea. The outlines of the New Agriculture Policy (NAP) are as follows:

- reorganization of the rural areas on the basis of the peasants having to take charge of their own fate;
- disengagement of the state through the gradual abolition of the agencies of intervention;
- a liberal input policy for groundnut seeds and fertilizers, whereby the peasants will now have to deal with the private sector and pay in cash; and
- a policy toward cereal grains using price incentives, aimed at achieving food self-sufficiency through the boosting of production.

In the final analysis, the NAP amounts to a total reversal of state policy inasmuch as its logic leads toward a complete withdrawal of the authorities from the rural areas. This would leave farmers – whose real incomes have fallen steadily since the early 1980s – altogether at a loss. It is understandable that the state can no longer afford to support the peasantry, but radical reforms ought to be introduced gradually, preceded by a transition period in which coherent, specific policies are defined.

Concern is all the greater because the Diama and Manantali dams on the Senegal River are nearing completion. These projects will eventually make it possible to irrigate a total of 350,000 hectares, at a projected pace of 4000 hectares annually through 1995, and 5000 hectares a year thereafter. At an average cost per hectare of 3.5 million CFA francs, such an effort implies annual financing needs of 14 billion CFA francs until 1995 and 17.5 billion a year in subsequent years. The logic of the NAP and structural adjustment implies that the peasants will have to take on development and operating costs, but until now irrigated farming was practised within the framework of structures wherein the farmer had few responsibilities. Even when farmers were in charge of the management and exploitation of lands, government agencies exercised supervision and were responsible for large-scale maintenance and equipment repair.

Finally, the abrupt and quasi-total withdrawal of the Senegalese state is incompatible with the harmonious and balanced development of the rural areas. The high cost of irrigated farming is likely to exclude poor peasants from access to land in favour of large private investors, both national and foreign. In other words, the abrupt implementation of structural adjustment in agriculture may well lead to a 'proletarianization' of small farmers and more pronounced inequalities in income and property. Such an evolution is likely to lead also to high levels of frustration among a rural population that accounts for 70 per cent of the working population of the country.

Employment and industrial policy

Based as they are on the notion that private initiative and free competition constitute the best guarantees for achieving efficiency in production, structural adjustment programmes run counter to the industrialization strategy pursued by Senegal since independence. This strategy had three main components:

- import substitution, with customs barriers to protect the principal industrial sectors;
- valorization and exploitation of local natural resources, such as groundnuts and phosphates; and
- a preponderant role for public enterprises or enterprises with public participation.

Structural adjustment has meant the development of a New Industrial Policy (NIP) along the following lines:

- implantation of high-value industrial branches with the aim of exporting to the markets of industrialized countries;
- privatization of all activities in which the private sector can replace the state, to the extent that this is not precluded by public-service considerations; and
- lowering of customs barriers in a rational way so as to subject local producers to sound competition.

The ways this new context for industrial policy affects the creation and destruction of jobs is illustrated by a recent survey published in *Africa International* that showed a degradation of employment in both the chemical and food-processing sectors (Table 5.4).

Table 5.4. Senegal, recent evolution of employment in two industrial branches

Branch	Expatriates		Africans		% Change	
	1988	1989	1988	1989	Expat.	Afric.
Chemicals	63	44	3021	2887	−19	−134
Food processing	94	78	10,532	10,226	−16	−306

Source: *Africa International*, No. 229, July–August 1990.

Reorientation of Senegal's industrial development was, of course, necessary. Despite protective customs barriers, most industries failed to make substantial productivity gains between independence and the 1980s. Five out of 18 industrial branches, accounting for 25 per cent of gross industrial value-added, saw the quantity of inputs per unit output grow between 1974 and 1982 (Kane, 1987). During the same period, labour productivity – as measured by the ratio of production over wage costs – declined in 13 of the 18 branches. The only significantly positive deviations from this pattern were in the clothing and leatherwork industry and in food processing; these were seen as the only sectors likely to create jobs.

In this low-productivity context, the opening of borders through the reduction of tariffs and abolition of the system of prior imports has compelled local enterprises to face international competition even though they are at a major disadvantage. The logic of adjustment forbids reliance on public subsidies, so restructuring leads immediately to an increase in urban unemployment. Moreover, the pace of urbanization in Senegal – as in other sub-Saharan African countries – is virtually double that of the industrialized world. Industrial activities are concentrated around Dakar and other major cities (especially Thies); these appear to rural populations no longer protected by the state to be privileged places where paying jobs can be found. More often than not this hope does not prove well-founded. But, in any case, rural incomes are in no way comparable to urban ones and such hopes do bring large numbers of people to the cities. Together, the consequences of structural adjustment for rural and urban zones rapidly result in the development of an urban informal sector, whose dynamism – praised by some experts – can be explained by the simple fact that it is subject to no fiscal, labour or other regulations.

Rationalization of public expenditures is also being carried out through a policy of early retirement to trim the state bureaucracy. This comes on the heels of a period when there has been a near-total freeze on public recruitment and when the number of higher education graduates entering the labour market is projected to reach 12,000 by 1990. All this will gradually inflate the number of educated young persons without hope of finding work, a potential source of social tension that could doom any structural adjustment programme to failure, however technically well done.

Conclusions

Structural adjustment programmes in Senegal correspond to a real need to correct economic and financial imbalances and misallocations of resources. But the short- and even medium-term social costs are extremely high and are quite likely to lead to social unrest, hindering the nonetheless inevitable processes of economic and financial reorganization. While 'the essence of economic development is structural adjustment' – as Paul Streeten has put it – the structures of industrialized countries 'are more stable and less subject to change' (Streeten, 1987). This suggests that liberalization measures ought to be designed in such a fashion that they can be applied gradually and thus avert abrupt changes that are socially inapplicable.

References

N. Hicks and A. Kubisch (n. d.). 'The Effect of Expenditure Reduction in Developing Countries.' Unpublished essay.

International Monetary Fund (1987). *Bulletin.* Washington DC.

K. Kane (1987). 'Reflexions on Senegal's New Industrial Bet.' Dakar: CREA, University Cheikh Anta Diop.

Paul Streeten (1987). 'Structural Adjustment: A Survey of the Issues and Opinions.' *World Development*, Vol. 15, No. 12.

World Bank (1989). *Sub-Saharan Africa: From Crisis to Sustainable Growth: A Long-Term Perspective Study.* Washington DC.

World Bank (1990). *World Development Report.* Washington DC.

6 Zambia

I. Mwanawina

Introduction

At independence in 1964, the United National Independence Party (UNIP) government of Zambia inherited an economic system geared towards the production of primary commodities, dominated by copper. The country lacked skilled manpower and technical know-how. Its geographical position and poor infrastructure made it unattractive to foreign investors.

Immediately after independence, the government followed a semi-liberal economic policy, with planning designed to stimulate growth by giving incentives to the private sector. These incentives consisted mainly of tariff protection and tax exemption which were based on an industry's net contribution to gross domestic product (GDP), diversification of the economy and creation of employment.

Largely due to the failure to attract private foreign investment and the lack of private indigenous Zambian entrepreneurship, the government started initiating and managing industrial projects through the Industrial Development Corporation (INDECO), which originated in the colonial period. The government's aim was to use INDECO until private buyers could be found for the projects.

During this period (1964 to 1969), the country prospered, with growth in real GDP (at constant 1980 prices) averaging 15 per cent (Table 6.1). The growth rate peaked in 1969 at 19 per cent, with a GDP of Kwacha 3123 million (US$4399 million). Per capita income also grew rapidly, averaging 13 per cent in the same period, and also peaking in 1969 at approximately K806 ($1127), a level that was never again achieved.

Primary production dominated other economic activities. Its contribution to GDP averaged about 48 per cent at constant 1965 prices, it contributed about 29 per cent to employment in the formal sector, and its growth rate averaged 10 per cent. Growth in the industrial sector, dominated by the construction industry, averaged 114 per cent. Electricity, gas and water grew at 116 per cent, and the other sectors at moderate rates of between 4 per cent and 9 per cent annually.

Subsequently, however, GDP growth stagnated at an average zero per cent in real terms over the 1970-85 period. Given the country's annual population growth rate of 3 per cent, per capita income declined at an average 6 per cent per year (Table 6.2). A study carried out by this author revealed that domestic factors were more important than external ones in explaining the country's poor economic performance, contrary to the general belief, and the government's view in particular.

Table 6.1. GDP and per capita income at constant 1980 prices 1964–9 (GDP in Kwacha million)

Year	GDP	Growth rate %	Per capita income	Growth rate %
1964	1618	18	450	–
1965	1915	18	566	26
1966	2172	13	643	14
1967	2449	13	676	5
1968	2632	7	665	–2
1969	3123	19	800	20
Average		15		13

Source: Mwanawina (1990).

Table 6.2. GDP and per capita income at constant 1980 prices 1970–85 (GDP in Kwacha million)

Year	GDP	Growth rate %	Per capita income	Growth rate %
1970	2766	–11	681	–15
1971	2769	0	535	–21
1972	3040	10	559	4
1973	3011	–1	624	12
1974	3211	7	668	7
1975	3135	–2	498	–25
1976	3271	4	497	0
1977	3114	–5	435	–12
1978	3172	2	414	–5
1979	2898	–9	429	4
1980	2986	3	438	2
1981	3253	9	455	4
1982	3161	–3	370	–19
1983	3099	–2	377	2
1984	3058	–1	339	–10
1985	3161	3	299	–12
Average		0		–5

Source: Mwanawina (1990).

Table 6.3. Contribution to GDP and employment by sectors at constant 1970 prices, 1970–83 (GDP in Kwacha million; employment in thousands)

Year	GDP	Total Employment	P. Prod. GDP	Emp.	Manu. GDP	Emp.	Elec. GDP.	Emp.
1970	1258	338	594	45	127	38	16	3
1971	1276	358	555	49	144	42	24	4
1972	1394	365	624	92	163	43	31	5
1973	1381	378	607	94	165	44	33	5
1974	1474	386	625	99	179	44	46	5
1975	1436	399	585	101	165	44	44	5
1976	1519	379	670	97	170	43	48	7
1977	1457	373	638	97	152	46	59	8
1978	1484	369	663	96	160	46	76	7
1979	1370	372	551	87	163	51	81	8
1980	1418	381	565	96	163	43	85	8
1981	1484	374	613	–	180	–	91	–
1982	1454	398	592	–	173	–	97	–
1983	1479	364	642	–	185	–	98	–
Average			43	23	11	12	4	2

Source: Mwanawina (1990).

The overall pattern of sectoral contribution to GDP remained the same, with changes only in the composition and magnitude of sectoral output (Table 6.3). The share of primary production decreased slightly to an average of 43 per cent, while the government sector compensated for this fall by increasing to an average of 13 per cent. The government sector also became the major employer, taking over from primary production, a position that has been maintained to the present time. Despite the declared objective of economic restructuring contained in almost all the national plans, the government has not succeeded in restructuring the economy. The country is still dominated by and geared towards the export of primary commodities.

In Zambia, three phases of economic adjustment can be identified:

- the liberal regime of the mid-1960s, from the time of independence in 1964 up to 1968;
- the period of economic nationalization from 1969 up to late 1991, corresponding to the second republic, with some attempts to liberalize the economy;
- the period of economic liberalization, which emerged with the reintroduction of plural politics, the electoral defeat of the UNIP, and the birth of the third republic in November 1991.

The country did not suffer from any balance of payments disequilibrium until 1971, when it drew on the International Monetary Fund's compensatory financing facility. In 1972, another drawing was made using the gold tranch. In both cases, the drawings were unconditional, given the understanding that the short fall in foreign revenue was temporary and would correct itself. In fact, the country did not need assistance from the IMF, as it had enough reserves. The IMF requested and encouraged the use of its resources, a classic example of faulty IMF advice to member countries.

As economic problems persisted with economic mismanagement, a piecemeal approach aimed at stabilizing the economy was agreed with the IMF under the first stand-by arrangement in 1976. The main condition attached to the facility was a downward adjustment of the exchange rate (devaluation), as the Fund was still advocating fixed exchange rates. The Kwacha was subsequently devalued by about 23 per cent.

For a long time, both the IMF and World Bank collaborated closely with the government in implementing dubious economic policies. By 1978 the IMF began to realize that the country's problems were both structural and due to mismanagement, a view that had been held by Zambian economists for quite a long time. Hence, in the stand-by arrangement of that year, liberalization of the economy was set as a condition. The government had no plans to privatize the once-private enterprises, which had by then become a burden to the taxpayers.

Increased efforts in the direction of economic liberalization were made in 1981 in close collaboration with the IMF, when the extended facility was first used. While the IMF had by now realized that the problem was mismanagement or maladjustment, government was not prepared to accept this, and also prohibited public debate on mismanagement or the deterioration of the economy in general. The only element of the programme which appeared to be implemented was a piecemeal devaluation of the currency within the framework of a fixed exchange rate regime whose basis was not generally known. It was evident, however, that no devaluation was in fact taking place, as inflation invariably ensured an appreciation of the local currency in real terms.

In 1984, the IMF continued to make frantic efforts to encourage economic liberalization when the third stand-by arrangement was made. The government even lined up a few enterprises for privatization. However, in the end, not a single enterprise was privatized. By this time, the IMF had shifted from advocating a fixed to a floating exchange rate regime. The Fund subsequently advised the government to float the currency through a system of weekly auctions which the domestic economy could not sustain and could only be kept in place by donor assistance. Price controls were removed and the government also agreed to a systematic reduction in the budget deficit, the root cause of excessive money supply and hence inflation.

In 1986, the fourth stand-by arrangement was made. Although the IMF praised Zambia as a success story for putting in place the instruments of economic restructuring, the government severed relations with the Fund, on the grounds that its conditions were too harsh. In October 1987, the Fund declared Zambia ineligible to use its financial resources because the country had failed to pay its obligations to the Fund, which stood at about US$900 million.

After the break-up with the IMF, the government pursued its own economic recovery programme for nine months. The aim was to tackle inflation, the budget deficit, the scarcity of essential commodities and the worsening levels of unemployment. The main difference between the IMF-supported adjustment programme and the government's 'go it alone' programme was the absence of privatization of the parastatals and liberalization of factor markets. One of the major weaknesses of the programme was its total dependence on foreign donors for funding, at a time when the donors were unwilling to support the programme in the absence of IMF and World Bank approval.

In order to attract donor assistance, the government drew up a Policy Framework Paper (PFP) for the 1989–93 period, which was endorsed by both the IMF and World Bank. The 'New Economic Recovery Programme: Economic and Financial Policy Framework 1991–3 (FPF)', provided the first review of the PFP and further elaborated the country's adjustment strategy up to 1993.

The main elements of the strategy include:

1   liberalization of agricultural pricing and marketing;
2   privatization and restructuring of parastatals;
3   introduction of trade and tariff reforms;
4   strengthening budgetary control;
5   rationalization of the mining sector.

The programme also included adherence to the Public Investment Programme (PIP), whose main thrust was to rehabilitate and maintain existing productive capacity and infrastructure, as well as a Social Action Programme designed to protect the most vulnerable groups from the effects of restructuring. In reality, no restructuring exercise has taken place (NCDP, 1991).

A dual foreign exchange system was introduced in February 1990 with the establishment of two windows. The first window rate was determined by the government, while it was claimed that the second window rate would be set approximately to the market clearing rate adjusted according to market conditions. However, it was also carefully managed by the government and was less than half the parallel market exchange rate.

In September 1991, the World Bank suspended the disbursement of funds to Zambia due to the country's failure to settle $20.8 million in arrears. The government was unable to pay the World Bank debt because donors had stopped their disbursement of funds for balance of payments support due to the government's failure to implement the PFP.

The government reacted by suspending all major projects in the PIP. In particular, the Social Action Programme, the agricultural extension research project, the mining technical assistance, privatization and education projects were cancelled. However, in delaying the implementation of the restructuring programme, the government also managed to lay a firm ground for the defeat of the ruling UNIP at the polls at the end of October 1991, in the first multiple party elections since 1968.

The Impact of the Adjustment Programme

Impact on health

The health sector was adversely affected by the government's excesses and economic mismanagement. The delivery of medical services had almost halted due to the shortage of drugs and equipment, and because poor conditions of service deterred qualified

Table 6.4. Government expenditure on health

Year	Total	% change	President (state house)	%[a] change	Health	%[a] change
1980	1,081,966		876		65,420	
1988	8,359,350		8496		648,074	
1989	9,700,990	16	21,725	120	895,802	19
1990*	26,946,453	178	52,659	−9	1,110,086	−55
Average change		98		56		−18

* Only up to September
Note[a]: Percentage change as a proportion of expenditure.
Source: CSO, *Monthly Digest of Statistics* (Series April/Sept. 1983; January/April 1986; August 1989; August 1990 and June 1991)
Government Printers, Lusaka.

Table 6.5. Major causes of mortality among adults in hospitals (15 years or over)

Major Causes	1987		1988		% change
	Number of deaths	% total	Number of deaths	% total	
Accidents & injuries	541	6	531	5	−2
Diseases of heart	1095	12	915	9	−6
Malignant, neoplasa & leukemia	438	45	1058	10	142
Respiratory disease	997	11	1228	12	23
Pulmonary tuberculosis	1209	13	280	3	−77
Genito-urinary system	115	1	555	5	38
Senility/ill-defined causes, excluding new born	598	6	188	2	−68
Ulcers/appendicitis, liver disorder	184	2	343	3	86
Non-infective gastro-intestinal disorders	445	5	572	6	29
Malaria	896	10	1298	14	45
Disorders of pregnancy/ delivery/ puerperium	216	2	199	2	−8
Disorders of skin/ subcutaneous tissue	88	1	101	1	15
Total Major	6822	73	7268	73	7
Total all cases	9283		10,120		9

Source: CSO (op. cit.).

medical personnel. Hospitals were saved from total collapse by both domestic and foreign donations. Furthermore, an inadequate transport system, compounded by the poor state of the roads, aggravated an already seriously run-down health sector. The Ministry of Health estimated that its fleet of vehicles had been reduced to less than half due to the unavailability of spare parts and poor maintenance.

Total government recurrent expenditure increased by 16 per cent in 1989 in nominal terms and more than doubled (178 per cent) by September 1990, an average annual increase of 98 per cent for the two years (Table 6.4). The president's expenditure more than doubled in 1989, by 120 per cent, while it marginally fell by 9 per cent in 1990, giving an average increase of 56 per cent. Yet for the health sector, expenditure increased by only 19 per cent in 1989 and declined drastically by 55 per cent in 1990, giving an average decline of 18 per cent. This indicates a shift in the government's priorities against health services, rather than the effect of a shortage of funds.

Between 1987 and 1988 the total number of recorded deaths increased by 9 per cent (Table 6.5), attributable to an increase in malaria cases. In the subsequent years, it rose to alarming proportions. For example, the University Teaching Hospital, the country's largest hospital, had an average of more than 20 deaths a day. At the hospital, patients slept on the floor and those who were fortunate to get beds had no bedding. The hospital did not have running water and most of the equipment was in poor working condition. The hospital did not have steam for sterilizing equipment. Sanitation was non-existent.

In early October 1991, all the operation theatres were closed down, except one for emergency cases, as they had become a health hazard to both medical personnel and patients. Some specialized clinics were also shut, while elsewhere in the country, two or more general hospitals were closed for similar reasons.

Impact on education

As in the case of the health sector, funding for education also declined steadily. Expenditure on the education sector increased in 1989 by 66 per cent, then drastically fell in 1990 by 20 per cent, giving an average increase of 44 per cent (Table 6.6). This, viewed against a marked increase in total expenditure averaging 97 per cent, again indicated a shift in government priorities rather than the effect of an across-the-board monetary squeeze resulting from the restructuring exercise.

Zambia has a population of about 8 million. With a growth rate of 3 per cent,

Table 6.6. Government expenditure on education

Year	Total	%Change	Education	% Change
1980	1,081,966		120,377	
1988	8,359,350		474,539	
1989	9,700,900	16	936,756	66
1990*	26,946,453	178	2,274,239	−20
Average		97		44

* Only up to September
Source: CSO (op. cit.).

funding of the sector for both capital and current expenditure should have increased in order to maintain educational standards.

The government set itself the objectives, among others, of providing learning materials, school desks and equipment, and reducing the level of illiteracy. However, there was a huge disparity between objectives and output. Over the years, no capital expenditure was incurred while recurrent expenditure experienced a disproportionate increase when compared with other sectors. The conditions of service for teachers deteriorated terribly and the educational infrastructure was severely run down to the point where pupils sat on floors without text books and other school facilities. Illiteracy was therefore on the upswing.

The non-existence of capital expenditure meant that classroom facilities lagged well below enrolment figures, resulting in large classes and overcrowding, particularly in primary schools. Secondary school places were only available to less than 20 per cent of those who completed their primary education, while higher education was available to an even smaller proportion.

Impact on employment

The labour force in Zambia accounts for about 30 per cent of the total population; it increased rapidly, at an average rate of 17 per cent, in the 1980–90 period (Table 6.7). However, faced with an ever-worsening economic crisis, the capacity of the productive sector to generate more jobs decreased over the years. The government reacted by absorbing more labour into the civil service, to the point where employment in community, social and personal services, which is dominated by the government itself, became the largest component of total formal employment (Table 6.7).

Hence formal employment increased marginally by only 1 per cent over the

Table 6.7. Formal employment by sector 1988–90

	1988	1989	1990*	% Change 1989–90
Agriculture, forestry & fisheries	37,380	37,860	39,000	14
Mining & quarrying	56,810	56,340	56,810	0
Manufacturing	49,940	50,340	50,940	1
Electricity & water	8720	8820	8940	1
Construction	29,830	29,350	29,060	−1
Distribution, restaurants & hotels	29,840	30,140	30,740	1
Transport & communications	25,020	25,320	23,650	−2
Finance, insurance, real estate & business services	23,360	23,780	24,180	1
Community, social & personal services	105,610	109,440	111,630	2
Total	369,390	371,840	376,950	1

* Preliminary
Source: CSO (op. cit.).

1988–90 period. Again, the government had set itself the objective of increasing employment as well as rehabilitating existing facilities within the framework of the FPF and PIP. However, the marginalization of capital spending over the years seriously inhibited increased employment in the formal sector. Unemployment stood at over 60 per cent for the whole period of 1985–90 (Table 6.8).

Table 6.8. Population and labour force 1980–90

	Pop. (million)	Urban pop. as % of total	Labour force (formal sector)	Unemployment %
1980	5.68	40	1.65	62
1985	6.72	45	1.99	64
1986	6.95	46	2.70	64
1987	7.15	48	3.74	64
1988	7.37	49	3.78	64
1989	7.57	50	3.82	63
1990*	7.79	51	3.86	62

* Provisional
Source: CSO (op. cit.).

Appendix 6.1

Exchange Rate, Kwacha to US$

1964–72	1973–75	1976	1977	1978–79	1980	1981	1982	
0.71	0.64	0.79	0.75	0.78	0.80	0.88	0.93	

1983	1984	1985	1986	1987	1988	1989	1990	1991*
1.51	2.20	5.70	12.70	8.00	10.00	12.90	28.99	52.49

* 1991 only 1st two quarters
Source: IMF (1990) *International Financial Statistics*, Washington DC: IMF; *International Financial Statistics Yearbook* (Series 1983, 1987 and 1988), Washington DC: IMF.

References

A. Martin (1975). *Minding Their Own Business: Zambia's Struggle Against Western Control*. London: Penguin Books.

Ministry of Finance and National Commission for Development Planning (1991). *New Economic Recovery Programme: Economic and Financial Policy Framework 1991–1993*. Lusaka: Government Printers.

I. Mwanawina (1990). *An Input–Output and Econometric Approach to Analysing Structural Change and Growth Strategies in the Zambian Economy*. Konstanz: Hartung-Gorre-Verlag.

National Commission for Development Planning (1981). *Economic Report*. Lusaka: Government Printers.

National Commission for Development Planning (1991). *Economic Report*. Lusaka: Government Printers.

7 Nigeria

Consequences for Employment

Tayo Fashoyin

Introduction

Although economic recovery measures had been applied in Nigeria since the beginning of the 1980s, a comprehensive set of restructuring policies was put in place only in September 1986. The aim was to achieve faster economic recovery and spur long-term development. This chapter assesses the impact of Nigeria's Structural Adjustment Programme (SAP) on employment, something that has been of considerable concern both to employers and to the government. After a brief overview of the Nigerian economy, with particular attention to the origins of the crisis, we present the major features of the adjustment measures. The next section examines the consequences of the SAP for employment, prices and inflation, wages and income, and social relations in workplace. Finally, we offer some conclusions and discuss the policy implications.

Profile of the Nigerian Economy

During the past two decades the Nigerian economy has undergone fundamental structural changes, with striking impact on employment and the labour force. While agriculture has historically been a key sector* – especially in terms of employment generation and food and raw materials production, the structure of the economy changed dramatically in the 1970s. The share of agriculture in the Gross Domestic Product (GDP) fell from 42 per cent in 1972 to 23 per cent in 1981, while manufacturing increased to 15.1 per cent in the same period. By 1980, manufacturing had reached a peak of 23 per cent of GDP.

This transformation was made possible by the phenomenal growth of crude oil extraction, which by 1972 was alone contributing 19 per cent of GDP. Oil accounted for only 2.6 per cent of the country's total exports in 1960; ten years later, this share jumped to 57 per cent, and today it stands at about 96 per cent. In the meantime,

---

* In 1960, agriculture contributed 64 per cent of Gross Domestic Product while manufacturing contributed only 3.1 per cent and mining (including petroleum) just 1.2 per cent (Federal Office of Statistics, 1966).

agriculture's share of exports plummeted from 86 per cent in 1960 to 4 per cent in 1975 and a mere 1 per cent in 1980 (Federal Office of Statistics, n.d.).

It is hardly surprising, then, that this sector has remained practically the sole source of government foreign exchange earnings, despite the sharp fall in world oil prices, rising steadily from 57.6 per cent in 1970 to 98.2 per cent in 1982 and maintaining the latter share throughout the subsequent decade. Moreover, oil earnings as a proportion of government revenue rose from 26 per cent in 1970 to 81 per cent in 1980 and remained at nearly 95 per cent in following years (Akatu and Olisadebe, 1987). Such phenomenal growth in foreign-exchange receipts underpinned the massive growth of the public sector, which accounted for some 50 per cent of GDP by the late 1980s. The government became the prime mover of the economy, investing large sums in social, infrastructural, and economic activities. As an illustration, some 200 public enterprises were established by the federal government, 110 of which were engaged in commercial undertakings (Omoruyi, 1987). Several more were created by each of the 19 states. Total government employment accounted for roughly 60 per cent of the modern sector.

Industrial employment – that is, in enterprises employing ten or more workers – stood at 1.8 million in 1964 and rose to 3.05 million in 1978, or 14.1 per cent of the labour force. By 1983, some 5 million were employed as wage-earners in the modern sector. (The figure excludes employment in the smallest enterprises and in the informal sector generally. As we shall see, the latter category encompasses far more workers than does the modern sector.)

Even so, agriculture continues to provide gainful employment for nearly 60 per cent of Nigeria's labour force. But while this sector persists in generating employment, its rate of growth averaged less than 1 per cent per annum between 1960 and 1980, well under the 3 per cent rate of population growth. The result has been a serious imbalance in food supply and demand, met in the 1970s by large imports of foodstuffs.

Unemployment remained quite low during the 1970s: about 4 per cent in the urban areas. Joblessness was concentrated among youths with poor education and lacking skills and experience. There was virtually no unemployment among university graduates and skilled workers (Diejomaoh, 1978).

Government oil revenues facilitated the introduction of generous employment policies in both sectors of the economy. The vast financial resources available in the public sector made feasible political programmes such as the creation of states and the establishment of government and parastatal enterprises. Such efforts led to the recruitment of a vast army of wage labour. In the private sector, a strategy of import-substitution industrialization in the 1960s and 1970s created manufacturing industries that required imports for up to 90 per cent of the raw-materials inputs (United Nations Industrial Development Organization, 1985). The industries so established generally operated behind high tariff barriers that insulated them from foreign competition. This combination of policies made it relatively easy for Nigerian enterprises to boost the level of waged employment, which in turn enlarged the domestic market for consumer goods (Akatu and Olisadebe, 1987). Furthermore, several wage awards were made to improve the conditions of workers whose salaries had been frozen or cut during the civil war of 1967–70. No less than five wage commissions acted between 1970 and 1981, and periodic awards were also made under incomes policy guidelines and the Minimum Wage Act of 1981. On this basis, the wages of the lowest-paid workers rose by more than 300 per cent during the 1970s (Fashoyin, 1986b: 137).

The economic crisis

The crunch came in mid-1981 with the collapse of the international oil market. Prices and production plummeted. Oil exports fell from 2.2 million barrels per day in 1979 to around 1.0 million per day in 1981–2 (Okongwu, 1987; Omoruyi, 1987: 29). Foreign exchange earnings, which had peaked at US$26 billion in 1980, fell to US$17.2 billion in 1981 and US$12.8 billion in 1982. By 1986, foreign-exchange earnings from oil amounted only to US$5.2 billion.

The oil crisis of the 1980s aggravated problems rooted in the ill-conceived economic policies of the 1970s, leading to a widening gap between falling foreign exchange revenue and mounting disbursements. Between June and December 1981 alone, the country's external reserves dropped from 5734.2 million naira to N2424.8 million (Table 7.1) (Aluko-Olokun, 1987). Desperately seeking to reverse the unfavourable economic climate, the Shagari administration in 1982 enacted the Economic Stabilization Act, which consisted largely of demand-management measures such as exchange controls, import restrictions, and other monetary and fiscal measures. The government next approached the International Monetary Fund for a loan, but negotiations stalemated until after the December 1983 coup d'état by General Buhari that removed President Shagari.

The Buhari administration imposed additional austerity measures, reducing capital and recurrent expenditures so as to stanch the public-sector deficit. These steps drastically reduced public employment as projects were abandoned and social-service outlays severely cut. The trend continued under the Babangida administration, which replaced Buhari following another coup in August 1985. A fifteen-month economic emergency was declared: to strengthen existing demand-management policies, deductions were ordered from employees' salaries and corporate profits. Further measures in early 1986, including the removal of petroleum subsidies, were aimed at persuading creditors to reschedule Nigeria's debts (Table 7.1). During that year the price of oil plummeted from US$28 a barrel to US$10; government revenues hence dropped by nearly 50 per cent. A decline in imports of 60 per cent nearly strangled the country's dependent industries.

The Structural Adjustment Programme

The oil boom of the 1970s helped to conceal the weakness of Nigeria's dependence on petroleum as the main engine of development. Moreover, it fostered a series of policies that embedded economic distortions and were in the long run inimical to self-reliant growth. These included import-substitution industrialization, which gave rise to an import-dependent manufacturing sector; ill-conceived and badly managed projects; and exchange controls and high tariffs (Phillips and Ndekwu, 1987; Akatu and Olisadebe, 1987). The danger of such a development path was concealed by the sudden deluge of oil earnings and the corresponding increases in government revenues.

It was this structural anomaly that economic recovery measures sought to correct. As noted above, several such steps were taken during 1982–6 on a largely *ad hoc* basis. The Structural Adjustment Programme, however, was a comprehensive package. It was introduced following the overwhelming public rejection of the IMF loan, which the Babangida administration transformed into a national debate upon coming to power in late 1985. The principle aims of the SAP were as follows:

1   to restructure and diversify the productive base of the economy so as to reduce dependence on the oil sector and on imports;
2   to achieve fiscal and balance-of-payments stability;
3   to lay the basis for sustainable, non-inflationary (or minimally inflationary) growth;
4   to improve the efficiency of the public sector, reduce the dominance of un-productive investments therein, and intensify the growth of the private sector (Federal Republic of Nigeria, 1986).

A key feature of the SAP has been its studied reliance on market forces to correct the perceived distortions in the economy, particularly the over-valuation of the naira. To achieve the latter objective, in September 1986 the Central Bank of Nigeria (CBN) began selling off available foreign exchange at bi-weekly auctions in the Foreign Exchange Market. The CBN also authorized interbank trading at market-determined rates to boost foreign-exchange inflow from non-oil sources. As a result, the value of the naira declined progressively from about N1.46=US$1 to N7.57=US$1 between September 1986 and June 1990 (Table 7.1). This downward adjustment has increased manufacturing costs owing to the high import content of that sector's products.

Deregulation also meant a new pricing policy: the removal of export controls, elimination of import-licensing schemes, abolition of marketing boards, deregulation of interest rates, and an end to price controls. Statutory limits on credit expansion were retained, however. Further, subsidies to domestic and international air fares, railway fares, freight charges, and petroleum products were substantially cut or eliminated. The prices of electricity and other such services increased by up to 500 per cent. Finally, government commenced in 1989 to sell off a large number of parastatal enterprises under the privatization provisions of the SAP. Many others are being commercialized, i.e., put on a for-profit basis. It will be seen below how some of these policies have led to a drastic fall in employment and living conditions and thus to conflicts between government and social groups in the country.

Impact of Adjustment Measures on Employment

Some caveats are in order before proceeding to a discussion of the impact of adjustment measures on employment. Despite the unique and controversial nature of the SAP, the information required for a thorough assessment is rather meagre. Data inputs for a study such as this one must come from a disparate range of sources. While much of the material necessarily comes from government sources, certain data are seriously lacking in continuity. Additional secondary data have been generated from other sources, such as trade unions and employers. In some cases, micro-level data have been

Table 7.1. Nigeria, selected macroeconomic indicators, 1983–1988

	1983	1984	1985	1986	1987	1988
Population (millions)	93.6	95.6	99.7	103.1	107.1	110.0
GDP, market prices (N bn)	62.6	70.0	78.8	79.7	110.6	137.0
Real GDP growth (%)	-8.5	-5.5	1.2	-2.1	1.7	4.2
GPD per capita (US$ bn)	770	730	800	640	370	300
Inflation (%)	23.2	9.6	5.5	5.4	10.2	38.3
Exports, FOB (US$ bn)	10.36	11.90	13.14	6.62	7.55	6.90
Imports, CIF (US$ bn)	12.30	9.40	7.92	4.44	4.46	4.60
External reserves (N mn)	881.70	1080.80	1641.10	3587.40	6007.00	n.a.
External debt (US$ bn)	16.59	18.66	19.52	24.47	28.71	29.50
Crude oil production (m bbl/day)	1.24	1.39	1.49	1.46	1.27	1.39
Average exchange rate (N/US$) (1990: N7.80=$1)	0.72	0.76	0.89	1.35	4.01	4.48

Source: Central Bank of Nigeria, *Annual Reports and Statements of Accounts,* various years; World Bank, *World Development Report,* various years; Economist Intelligence Unit, *Nigeria, Country Profile,* various issues.

Table 7.2. Redundancies in Nigerian industries, 1983

Industry group	Number responding	Total labour force	Redundancies	Redundancies as % of total labour force
Chemical	26	10,467	2	0.02
Shop and distributive	12	9835	844	8.58
Banks and insurance	12	3149	0	0
Food and beverages	10	7822	22	0.28
Metal products	8	3594	194	5.39
Paper products	7	2976	680	18.92
Petroleum	7	1818	174	9.57
Construction	6	3810	732	19.21
Shipping	5	2149	134	6.23
Precision electrical	5	1634	147	8.99
Automobile	4	4199	0	0
Textile and garment	4	3002	45	1.49
Leather and footwear	3	2096	0	0
Printing and publishing	3	1044	56	5.36
Furniture and fixtures	2	302	48	15.89
Air services	1	413	14	3.38
Totals	116	58,310	3306	5.66

Source: *Survey on Redundancy and Closures.* Lagos, Nigeria Employers' Consultative Association. January 23, 1984, p.2.

gathered from private-sector organizations. So it should be borne in mind that the information presented here is far from perfect, although it does give a reasonably good picture of the SAP's overall impact on employment.

Quite apart from the question of data, the three years of SAP implementation may seem a relatively short time-span from which to draw definitive conclusions as to its consequences. Moreover, some of the adjustment measures that are bound to have monumental effects on employment (such as privatization and commercialization) are still being implemented at this writing. And some of the effects examined here may turn out to be short-run results that will change significantly over a longer timespan. Despite these reservations, there is sufficient evidence to allow some conclusions, however tentative, as to the effects of adjustment measures on the labour force.

Our evaluation of the impact of adjustment measures, then, will focus on four interrelated themes: employment and unemployment, consumer prices and inflation, wages and incomes, and social relations in the workplace. While this selection may appear eclectic or arbitrary, it represents, in our view, the broader context in which the employment consequences of the economic recovery measures ought to be examined.

Employment and unemployment

Of a labour force of 32.2 million people in 1980, 30.8 million were gainfully employed. Of these, some 18.5 million, or 60 per cent, were engaged in agriculture, but only a small proportion of the latter (8.7 per cent) worked for wages. The majority in the rural areas were to be found in small-scale or peasant agriculture, but the growth of the urban sector and increasing industrialization have reduced the weight of this category (Federal Ministry of National Planning, 1981: 426). Indeed, about 10 per cent of the labour force was employed for wages in 1980, in establishments of all sizes. Various estimates have suggested that by 1985 about 15 per cent of the labour force would have been in wage employment had the economy not run into difficulties.

Throughout the 1970s boom, industrial enterprises were major generators of employment. Though manufacturing accounted for only 6 per cent of GDP, it employed some 14 per cent of the labour force at its peak in 1984. This suggests that any development that adversely affected the capacity of industries to maintain production was bound to have deleterious consequences for employment. It is thus not surprising that deregulation and the abolition of exchange controls and tariffs have led to marked declines in industrial job opportunities.

The official estimate of overall unemployment was 4.4 per cent of the labour force in 1980; the rate rose to 10 per cent in 1986 and 12.2 per cent in 1987. These appear to be conservative estimates, and a figure of the order of 15 per cent would seem more realistic. The unreliability of official statistics is demonstrated by contradictory government statements on the unemployment problem. On one hand, it has been asserted that unemployment declined from 7.4 per cent in 1987 to 4.7 per cent in 1988; on the other, government acknowledged in 1988 that improvements in agriculture and industry and the programmes of the National Directorate of Employment 'had no discernible impact on the unemployment situation' (*The Guardian*, 4 September 1989).

In the 1960s and 1970s, the overwhelming majority of unemployed were young people below 24 years of age, generally poorly educated, untrained, and inexperienced.

If unemployment hardly existed then among university graduates, in the 1980s this became a serious social problem. A government survey indicated that graduate unemployment rose from 4 per cent in 1981 to 6.4 per cent in 1985 (Federal Office of Statistics, 1985). The Committee of Vice-Chancellors asserted around the same time that between 55,000 and 60,000 graduates were unemployed (*The Guardian*, 15 March 1986).

Rising official unemployment levels only begin to suggest the SAP's less than satisfactory short-term impact in stemming the wave of redundancies and job losses. According to the Manufacturers Association of Nigeria (MAN), some 40 per cent of the industrial workforce was retrenched or made redundant in 1984–6 (MAN, 1988). This is corroborated by data on installed capacity utilization, which stood at 43.6 per cent in 1984 but fell to between 35 per cent and 38 per cent in 1986–7 (CBN, 1985: 38; CBN, 1987: 16). In heavily import-dependent industries such as electronics, automobiles, sugar confectionery, paints, and beer, installed capacity was utilized at less than 20 per cent during the period. Overall, the MAN estimated that capacity utilization remained at an average of 37.5 per cent in 1988, and noted, too, that industrial closures were being reported (MAN, 1988).

Reduced industrial capacity has led to widespread dismissals and lay offs. Table 7.2 indicates the extent of redundancies during 1983. Hardest hit were construction, paper products, and furniture and fittings. Other groups such as shop and distributive, petroleum, and precision and electrical have also experienced high redundancy rates. Table 7.3 gives the occupational classification of those who lost their jobs in the food, beverage, and tobacco industry in 1983–4. This information is particularly useful in that it depicts the types of personnel who have been thrown into the jobless queue. While more current data are not available, all indications point to persisting redundancy. The manufacturing sector accounted for 24.7 per cent of all redundancies during 1982–3, and 6.2 per cent of the sector's workforce was made redundant during 1984–5. Construction, where the recession had a more devastating impact, accounted for 37 per cent of all redundancies in 1982–3; 42 per cent of the construction workforce was made redundant in 1984–5 (Fashoyin, 1989).

Further evidence of the magnitude of the unemployment situation is presented in Table 7.4, which shows the registration of jobless persons at employment agencies, vacancies reported, and placements made. The latter category illustrates the limited absorptive capacity of establishments in the modern sector, and the gap between vacancies and placements reflects the extent of capacity under-utilization. (In assessing the merit of this table, it should be borne in mind that both registration by unemployed persons and reports of vacancies by employers are voluntary; the table at best indicates the order of magnitude of the problem.)

While detailed statistics are not available for the public sector either, estimates suggest that about a million workers may have been 'retired' (a euphemism for redundancy) since 1984. The trend in the public sector has recently gained momentum, as the federal and state governments embark on privatization and commercialization. In 1989, Nigeria Airways, earmarked for privatization, reduced its workforce by 60 per cent, while the Nigeria Railway Corporation, undergoing commercialization, cut its workforce of more than 10,000 by 34 per cent. The unemployment effect of such adjustment measures has been mitigated by the large absorptive capacity of the

Table 7.3. Nigeria, redundancies in food, beverage, and tobacco industry, 1983–1984

Occupational Category	Number
Sales representatives	59
Fitters/mechanics	89
Marketing and sales (management grade)	21
Accountants	9
Engineers	13
Confidential secretaries/typists	19
Personnel and administrative staff	18
Nurses and midwives	8
Production supervisors/managers	31
Drivers	14
Storekeepers/managers	25
Food technologists/quality-control managers	9
Total	311

Source: Association of Food, Beverage and Tobacco Employers, Lagos, 1984.

Table 7.4. Nigeria, registered unemployment and vacancies, 1984–88

Grade	1984	1985	1986	1987	1988
Lower Grade:					
Total registration	114,190	92,712	85,158	145,084	116,162
Vacancies	9836	7609	13,050	16,502	14,154
Placements	3865	2024	2378	4988	2506
Professional and Executive:					
Total registration	n.a.	n.a.	6123	15,100	16,759
Vacancies	n.a.	n.a.	606	444	591
Placements	n.a.	n.a.	148	175	282

Source: Central Bank of Nigeria, *Annual Reports and Statement of Accounts, 1987–88.*

Table 7.5. Nigeria, price changes in selected food items, 1981–1989, current Nairas

Food Item	1981	1986	1989	% Change 1981/86	% Change 1986/89
Rice (50 kg)	30.00	180.00	650.00	500	261
Elubo (yam powder, 1 tin)	6.00	18.00	45.00	200	150
Palm oil (4 litres)	4.00	12.00	29.00	200	142
Tomatoes (1 tin)	0.25	0.80	1.80	220	125
Fish (carton)	25.00	85.00	200.00	240	135
Chicken (carton)	25.00	80.00	182.00	220	128
Egg (one)	0.10	0.30	0.80	200	167
Yam (1 tuber)	0.50	2.50	7.00	400	180
Plaintain (bunch)	2.00	5.00	22.00	150	340
Tea/coffee (1 packet/25 bags)	0.25	0.80	3.25	220	306

Source: J. E. Odah, 'SAP and the Living Condition of Nigerian Workers', unpublished memo, Lagos: Nigeria Labour Congress, 1989.

informal sector and agriculture, but these also face high jobless rates and low incomes.

The government has acknowledged the seriousness of the unemployment problem and has taken extensive measures in recent years to deal with it. The National Directorate of Employment (NDE) was established in 1987, with substantial budgetary allocations to create job opportunities for all categories of unemployed persons. The NDE has developed four programmes:

1 a national youth employment programme, in which the National Open Apprenticeship Scheme and the Vocational Skill Development Scheme form the core;
2 the Special Public Works Programme, which provides for the employment of both graduates and non-graduates in the maintenance of public institutions;
3 the Agricultural Development Scheme, for unemployed graduates; and
4 the Small-Scale Industries Programme, which provides technical and financial resources to young entrepreneurs and those who have lost their jobs because of economic contraction.

Although these programmes await comprehensive evaluation, there is no doubt that they have helped to reduce the rate of increase in unemployment and have thereby diffused the social tension that is naturally associated with high levels of joblessness. Indeed, to the extent these programmes have promoted the concept of self-employment, they have helped draw attention to the oft-ignored informal sector. Nigerian experience has shown that the latter has a remarkable absorptive capacity for employing both large numbers of young persons and skilled and experienced workers who have lost their jobs as a result of economic crisis. Estimates show that the urban informal sector employs between 15 per cent and 20 per cent of the total labour force today.

Prices and inflation

The phenomenal increase in consumer prices, resulting from the precipitous drop in the value of the naira, has been the most immediate and visible effect of the adjustment programme. The high cost of foreign exchange has resulted in high prices for both locally produced and imported raw-materials inputs. Ironically, the official price index does not attest to the galloping price hikes in most instances. The credibility of these statistics is called into question by the dramatic drop in inflation asserted between 1984 and 1985, from 39.6 per cent to 5.5 per cent, despite obvious price trends. Prices for accommodation and fuel are said to have risen by 40.6 per cent in 1986, and those for household goods by 30.8 per cent. Increases for these items were generally lower in 1987, though inflation virtually doubled that year. The 1988 figures show inflation at a rate of 38.2 per cent, but a more realistic estimate would be over 50 per cent. Table 7.5 offers a more accurate representation of observable trends in price movements (though even this evidence has serious methodological weaknesses).

Good harvests and increased agricultural production in some years did result in a deceleration of prices, particularly in 1985–6. The overall upward trend, including for food items, can be explained in part by the combined effects of adjustment policies. For example, the removal of export controls and the downward adjustment of the naira increased farmgate prices of cash crops (cocoa, cotton, rubber, coffee, palm produce), inducing a shift to their production. While this led to a certain improvement in non-oil export earnings (from about US$0.48 billion in 1987 to US$1 billion in 1988), it had adverse effects on production of food crops and hence on food prices (Omoruyi, 1987: 32). Additionally, industries producing for the domestic market are continually increasing their use of local inputs and are thus in competition with consumers for such staples as sorghum and maize, thereby boosting demand for these popular food items.

The cost of transportation by both air and land has increased astronomically in response to the downward adjustment of the naira. Air fares, both local and international, increased by between 250 and 400 per cent in 1986–9. The steep rise in the price of vehicles has made daily commuting extremely costly for urban workers in Lagos, Kaduna, Ibadan, and Enugu. A Peugeot saloon car, widely used as a taxi, cost N9000–N12,000 in 1985, but N120,000–N180,000 in 1989. And the Bedford lorry (or *molue* in Lagos), used for mass transit in urban areas, cost up to N300,000 in 1989. These prices induced the National Union of Road Transport Workers to announce a 300 per cent fare increase in June 1989 (*Business Concord*, 13 June 1989).

While the rural sector has been hit by declining or unstable prices for agricultural products, the internal terms of trade have shifted in favour of farmers. Farmgate prices of most products have increased since the adjustment measures went into effect. Cocoa prices rose from N1600 per ton in 1986 to N15,000 per ton at the end of 1988, an increase largely due to deregulation. Available evidence suggests that this performance by the agricultural sector has rekindled interest in agricultural employment, although the overall trend probably continues to decline in favour of the urban sector. Improved performance in agriculture has perhaps also narrowed rural–urban differentials, particularly in view of the near-stagnation of urban incomes. But while the cash income of farmers has increased, deregulation has forced up prices for consumer goods and thus dampened any effect on real income.

Incomes and the real wage

The burden of structural adjustment falls heaviest on those on fixed incomes: wage and salary earners in urban areas. Real earnings have fallen significantly as a result of a prolonged wage freeze (1983–7) and a series of cuts in workers' wages and benefits. Cutbacks in benefits to public employees began in 1984, and compulsory wage deductions of between 2 per cent and 20 per cent were transferred to an Economic Recovery Fund (Circular No. B63304, 21 December 1984). Additional deductions were forced on employees at the state level. Kwara State transferred 10 per cent of salaries to an industrial development levy, and Lagos State levied N20 for development from every taxable adult in 1989. Niger State suspended benefits to workers, and several other states simply reneged on payments of salaries and benefits.

The wage freeze was lifted in 1988 and collective bargaining resumed in the private sector. Wages for public-sector workers were raised by 15 per cent and benefits increased by up to 200 per cent. Comparable adjustments were achieved in the private sector through bargaining. In the end, private–public differentials had increased substantially, to about 3:1 at the lower levels and much higher still at the top of the occupational structure. Even so, an assessment of the impact of the 1988 increases on real income must take into account the fact that consumer prices rose 32.7 per cent in

Table 7.6. Nigeria, nominal and real wages of lowest-paid workers, 1980–9

Year	Basic nominal wage (naira)	% Change	Real wage (naira)	% Change
1980	1200	–	1200.0	–
1981	1224	2.0	1012.8	–15.6
1982	1500	22.6	1152.7	+13.8
1983	1524	1.6	950.4	–17.6
1984	1548	1.6	691.6	–27.2
1985	1572	1.6	665.6	–3.8
1986	1596	1.5	641.3	–3.7
1987	1620	1.5	590.8	–7.9
1988	1860	14.8	290.6	–17.0
1989	1980	6.5	370.7	–24.4

Source: Computed from data of the Federal Office of Statistics and the Federal Civil Service Commission, Lagos.

the six months after the freeze was lifted; the food price index rose 44.5 per cent in the same period. Comparable figures for the preceding six months were 7 per cent and 8.9 per cent respectively (Fashoyin, 1988).

The overall effect – continuing decline in real wages – can be seen in Table 7.6, column 5. This attests to the strength of inflation and the inability of periodic hikes in money wages to improve real living standards for workers. Moreover, while non-wage benefits were generously increased in 1988, bringing total annual compensation for the lowest-paid worker to N4578 in nominal terms, real total compensation actually fell from N1207.40 in 1988 to N886.30 in 1989. Such failures to cope with sky-rocketing inflation have fortified the resolve of the Nigeria Labour Congress (NLC) to seek a revision in the minimum wage from N125 to N1490 per month. At this writing, a Tripartite Committee is examining the NLC demand.

Individually, many urban wage and salary earners in both sectors are finding supplementary means of livelihood. A good number engage in 'straddling', performing additional income-generating activities, usually in the informal sector. Others have taken to farming, growing food items such as vegetables, maize, yams, and cassava, the prices of which have gone beyond affordable limits (Table 7.5).

Relations in the workplace

The impact of adjustment measures on employment cannot be fully grasped without an examination of the degree of social consensus among partners in industry. It can be said at the outset that when jobs are threatened – as has been the case in Nigeria since the early 1980s – trade unions become restive and defensive. Without a certain degree of understanding between unions and employers, there is bound to be considerable conflict in workplaces. On the other hand if it is assumed that the restructuring of the economy for long-term development is inevitable, then antagonism between labour and management will not be conducive to the optimizing of opportunities for such adjustment.

As might have been expected, the contraction of employment adversely affected the organizational strategies of the trade unions, placing them on the defensive and making them more vulnerable to employers' workforce reduction strategies. All unions lost membership, with the possible exception of those in financial institutions. Aggregate membership declined from 1.4 million in 1982 to 1.2 million in 1987, a drop of 14 per cent.

A look at specific industries will provide a clearer picture of the seriousness of the problem. In construction, union membership fell from 160,000 in 1982 to 35,000 in 1987, or 78.1 per cent. The textile union lost 60 per cent of its 200,000 members between 1979 and 1984. Among public employees, the Civil Service Technical Workers Union (second largest in the sector) lost nearly 24 per cent of its 122,274 members in 1984–7, while the Nigerian Ports Authority Workers Union lost 51.1 per cent of its 40,400 members in 1983–7 (all statistics from Office of the Registrar of Trade Unions, Federal Ministry of Employment, Labour and Productivity, Lagos).

Membership decline has disorganized the unions, especially in their ability to challenge the severe abuses inflicted by some employers under the guise of structural adjustment measures. It has also undermined union solidarity, fuelling factional disputes within several unions and occasionally disrupting labour–management relations (Imoisili, 1986: 81–7). Such tensions undermine the constructive contribution that unions can make to socio-economic development at a time of structural adjustment.

On the whole, continuing loss of employment has led rather to a moderation in union activities and changes in strategy. Since the recession, several unions have shown keen interest in collaborating with employers to seek genuinely less painful alternatives to redundancies, lay-offs, and declining incomes (Fashoyin, 1986a: 42–59). During the past five years several unions have agreed to a freeze on wages and/or benefits, review of work rules to give management a freer hand in personnel utilization, reduction in hours worked, and, in some cases, outright cuts in wages and/or benefits.

In the Kaduna Textiles Company, the impact of recession severely reduced the firm's ability to import raw materials and spare machine parts. This led to serious workers' riots in 1984, but agreements were eventually reached to reduce wages by 25 per cent while some benefits were cut, frozen, or totally abolished. At the Peugeot Automobile Plant, the workforce of 3000 was reduced by half in 1986; those who remained took cuts in working hours and had benefits decreased or abolished. Employers for the most part extended job security in return for such concessions.

Available evidence clearly suggests that these efforts by unions and management have been short-term in character. As adjustment measures failed to produce perceptible long-term effects, many companies that had signed concession agreements ultimately resorted to redundancies or lay-offs. Cadbury, for instance, was able to maintain its workforce in this fashion in 1984–6 but ultimately retrenched in 1987 (Ogunyolu, 1984; Oloyede, 1988).

Social relations in the public sector have been far less satisfactory. While a few unions voluntarily gave up rights as a trade-off for job security – as in a recent undertaking by the Nigerian Union of Railwaymen to relinquish members' non-wage benefits rather than face further redundancies – the more common approach in this sector has been for employers to cut benefits unilaterally or cancel them outright (*West Africa*, 28 August – 3 September 1989). In the railway case mentioned, the union's offer to freeze members' benefits was turned down by the corporation. Evidence indicates, moreover, that reductions in compensation in the public sector were not generally intended to save jobs but rather to reduce the employers' wage bill. The problem is compounded by employers' (i.e., governments') frequent delinquency in the payment of wages and benefits when due.

Several policies do exist to mitigate the unfavourable effects of adjustment measures on employment. Agricultural policies are expected to cushion the effects of declining incomes and living standards and to provide the jobless with gainful employment. This has indeed had a favourable impact, given the improvements seen in this sector in the past three years.

After the May 1989 riots the government announced a package of relief measures meant to cushion the hardships brought about by adjustment measures (*The African Guardian,* 19 June 1989; *West Africa,* 26 June – 2 July 1989). These included duty-free importation of commercial vehicles to ease the chronic problem of urban mass transportation. Facilities of US$30 million were promised for the importation of spare parts for automobiles and industry. The National Directorate of Employment was ordered to create 62,000 jobs, and the Ministry of Works was mandated to create 460 jobs in each of the 21 states (9660 total). Schools were directed to fill all teaching vacancies and to establish farms in a bid to boost food production. And foreign exchange was made more accessible to pharmaceutical firms for the importation of drugs.

Conclusions and Policy Implications

As should now be evident, adjustment measures generally have had an unfavourable impact on employment, especially in the short run. Nonetheless, the introduction of adjustment policies appears inevitable if the anomalies of previous economic mismanagement are to be removed and if the foundations for long-term development are to be laid. In the process, however, employment opportunities have been reduced, leading to a severe decline in workers' living standards, especially in the modern sector.

This explains why the commitment of government to alleviating widespread unemployment has gathered momentum in recent years. The productive sectors of the economy should continue to be given every encouragement and assistance to generate jobs, however. The role of these sectors cannot be overestimated, bearing in mind the conventional labour-market postulate that the demand for labour is a derived one, dependent upon demand for goods and services produced. Therefore, policies aimed at stimulating demand for labour must be related to measures designed to boost the level of economic activity. In other words, provision of jobs to the large numbers of unemployed persons depends on rapid economic recovery.

The National Directorate of Employment (NDE) has developed programmes to create jobs in both the short and long terms. But its capacity to do so depends both on the quality of these programmes and on whether the beneficiaries thereof really constitute the target population. Success also depends on the size of budgetary allocations the NDE receives. Finally, the NDE ought to ensure appropriate linkages between its own programmes and those of other social-development agencies.

The informal sector has demonstrated that it can serve as employer of last resort, and there is no doubt that its job-generating capacity has outstripped that of the modern sector in recent years. This trend is very likely to continue in the 1990s; thus public policy ought to be directed toward this highly important sector. There is a need for research on its nature and characteristics, and on whether old definitions still accurately depict the phenomenon. Greater understanding of the nature of employment conditions in the informal sector is also needed, as well as a thorough grasp of the linkages between it and the formal sector.

References

P. A. Akatu and E. U. Olisadebe (1987). 'Management of the Nigerian Economy'. *Economic and Financial Review*, Vol. 25, No. 4: 54–66.

Isaac Aluko-Olokun (1987). 'An Appraisal of the Second-Tier Foreign Exchange Market (SFEM)'. In Adedotun O. Phillips and Eddy C. Ndekwu, eds, *Structural Adjustment Programme in a Developing Economy: The Case of Nigeria*. Ibadan: Nigerian Institute of Social and Economic Research.

Central Bank of Nigeria (1985). 'A Review of Business Activity, January–June 1985'. *Economic and Financial Review*, Vol. 23, No. 3.

——(1987). 'Performance of the Manufacturing Sub-sector during the First Quarter of 1987'. *Economic and Financial Review*, Vol. 25, No. 1.

V. P. Diejomaoh (1978). 'The Employment Experience and Prospects of Nigerian University Graduates'. In U. G. Damachi and K. Ewusi, eds, *Manpower Supply and Utilization in West Africa*. Geneva: International Institute for Labour Studies.

Tayo Fashoyin (1986a). 'Collective Bargaining Challenges during Economic Recession'. In Ukandi G. Damachi and Tayo Fashoyin, eds, *Contemporary Problems in Nigerian Industrial Relations*. Lagos: Development Press.

——(1986b). *Incomes and Inflation in Nigeria*. London and Lagos: Longman.

——(1988). 'Wages and Salaries Review in the Public and Private Sectors of the Nigerian Economy since the Lifting of Wage Freeze'. Unpublished paper, presented to Workshop on Incomes Policy in a Structurally Adjusted Economy; Productivity, Prices and Incomes Board, 26–27 October 1988.

——(1989). 'Economic Recession and Employment Security in Nigeria'. Unpublished paper, presented to Faculty of Business Seminar, McMaster University, 3 April 1989.

Federal Ministry of National Planning (1981). *Fourth National Development Plan, 1981–5*.

Federal Office of Statistics (n.d.). *Annual Abstract of Statistics*. Lagos.

——(1976). *National Accounts of Nigeria*. Lagos.

Federal Office of Statistics (1985). *Labour Force Sample Survey*.

Federal Republic of Nigeria (1986). *Structural Adjustment Programme for Nigeria, July 1986 to June 1988*. Lagos: Government Printer.

I. C. Imoisili (1986). 'The Effects of Inter-Union Trade Disputes on Enterprise Labour Relations: Options for Employers'. In ed., *AFBTE in 1986*. Lagos: Association of Food, Beverage and Tobacco Employers.

Manufacturers Association of Nigeria (1988). *MAN Half-Yearly Economic Review*, No. 3, January–June 1988.

A. A. Ogunyolu (1984). 'An Assessment of Labour-Management Cooperative Efforts in a Recessionary Economy: A Case Study of Cadbury Nigeria Limited'. Unpublished M.Sc. dissertation, Department of Industrial Relations and Personnel Management, University of Lagos.

C. S. P. Okongwu (1987). 'Review and Appraisal of the Structural Adjustment Programme, July 1986 to June 1987'. Lagos (unpublished mimeo).

A. O. Oloyede (1988). 'Human Resource Management in a Recessionary Economy: The Case of Cadbury Nigeria Limited'. Unpublished M.Sc. dissertation, Department of Industrial Relations and Personnel Management, University of Lagos.

S. E. Omoruyi (1987). 'A Review of the Structural Adjustment Programme, the Foreign Exchange Market and Trade Policies in Nigeria'. *Economic and Financial Review*, Vol. 25, No. 4: 29–33.

Adedotun O. Phillips and Eddy C. Ndekwu (1987). *An Appraisal of the Second-Tier Foreign Exchange Market (SFEM)*. Ibadan: Nigerian Institute of Social and Economic Research.

United Nations Industrial Development Organization (1985). *Industrial Development Review Series, Nigeria*.

8 Nigeria
Consequences for Health

Deji Popoola

Introduction

Perhaps the most dramatic effects of Nigeria's structural adjustment programme have been manifested in the area of health and health care. There have been markedly adverse direct consequences in terms of access to health services and the nutritional status of mothers and children, while the sharply rising costs of housing, food, transportation, and other basic needs have likewise resulted in a deterioration in physical well-being. Indeed, most Nigerians find themselves engaged in a battle for survival.

This report on health and structural adjustment in Nigeria will first discuss the population situation and then take up the federal government's budget projections for health care during 1985–90. Based on these data and the disease pattern for the 1984–8 period, some conclusions as to the impact of structural adjustment on health and health care will be drawn.

Population

The most recent data indicate that Nigeria's birth rate has remained fairly constant at about 50 per 1000 population during the past 15 years, while the death rate has been cut in half. In terms of population growth, this has meant a rise in the rate of natural increase from 2.1 per cent in 1950 to 3.3 per cent in 1985. At the current rate, the population is projected to double in approximately 20 years. Between 1984 and 1988 alone the population grew from an estimated 98,563,300 to 112,258,000.

Because birth rates have been so high for so long, the population is relatively quite young, with some 47 per cent under the age of 15. Such a high dependency rate is quite significant when the adverse effects of structural adjustment are taken into account.

The Health Care Budget

Budgetary allocations to health care have been far below the financial requirements of this sector, falling drastically short of the target of 5 per cent of national budget advocated by the World Health Organisation. In 1982 – even before the onset of structural adjustment – the federal government was spending only US$0.42 per capita on health, a sum that did not even suffice to pay for the treatment of one attack of malaria in a country where the average citizen is likely to experience multiple malaria attacks annually. Per capita allocation in the 1990 budget amounted to US$0.62, again, not enough even to purchase a single packet of Nivaquine malaria remedy. It is thus apparent that individuals heavily subsidize their health care needs.

Rising living costs and unemployment brought on by structural adjustment have led to sharp reductions in calorific and protein intake among the bulk of the population. Not only have the prices of high-protein foods such as fish and meat become prohibitive, but even staple carbohydrates such as yam and cassava have been placed beyond the reach of many of the poor. Indeed, a bag of rice now sells for between N500 and N800, more than a month's salary for the average worker. With the national minimum wage at N125 per month, a bag of rice thus costs between four and five times the monthly wage of the lowest-paid worker.

Table 8.1. Nigeria, approved budget for health, 1985–90 (Naira)

Year	Recurrent	Capital
1985	167,726,570	56,053,145
1986	279,225,970	81,200,000
1987	166,895,780	69,545,320
1988	259,938,460	100,734,000
1989	326,638,700	121,000,000
1990	401,136,010	180,000,000

Source: Federal Ministry of Health, Statistical Division, Lagos, 1990.

The Pattern of Disease

Deteriorating diets have led to lowered resistance to disease among wide sectors of the population. Indeed, ailments that had been declared completely eradicated, such as smallpox and guineaworm infestation, have reappeared in recent years. Recorded cases of malaria increased from 1.2 million in 1984 to 1.8 million in 1988, and most other notifiable diseases have shown yearly increases as well (Table 8.2).

In the countryside, water-borne diseases in particular have become more prevalent owing to the government's inability to fund the maintenance of boreholes and water wells. Where guineaworm infestation has been severe, entire households have been affected and peasant farmers have had to abandon their farms. As for urban areas, old wells that had filled up with waste materials when pipe-borne water was available have had to be re-dug as a source of household water. Lack of availability of necessary chemicals has meant a deterioration in the quality of water supplied from government-run treatment plants.

Childhood diseases such as measles and whooping cough have also become more

Table 8.2. Nigeria, major causes of morbidity from selected notifiable diseases, 1984–1988

	1984		1985		1986		1987		1988	
	Cases (x1000)	Rate per 1000 pop.	Cases (x1000)	Rate per 1000 pop.	Cases (x1000)	Rate per 1000 pop.	Cases (x1000)	Rate per 1000 pop.	Cases (x1000)	Rate per 1000 pop.
Malaria	1242	1261	1284	1261	1020	970	1108	1021	1775	1046
Dysentery	223	226	259	254	186	177	235	216	221	197
Pneumonia	1015	103	1202	118	82	78	88	81	95	84
Measles	1226	185	162	159	116	110	78	71	56	68
Gonorrhoea	55	56	71	69	42	40	64	59	42	37
Whooping cough	63	64	92	91	42	40	51	47	35	31
Schistosomiasis	37	37	32	31	27	26	31	29	33	29
Tuberculosis	11	11	15	15	14	13	20	18	17	15
Chicken pox	66	67	76	75	21	20	14	13	15	13
Viral influenza	6	6	18	17	10	10	13	12	14	12

Source: Department of Planning, Research and Statistics, Federal Ministry of Health, Lagos, 1990.

Table 8.3. Nigeria, major causes of death from selected notifiable diseases, 1984–1988

| | 1984 | | 1985 | | 1986 | | 1987 | | 1988 | |
	Deaths	Rate per 1000 pop.	Deaths	Rate per 1000 pop.	Deaths	Rate per 1000 pop.	Deaths	Rate per 1000 pop.	Deaths	Rate per 1000 pop.
Malaria	773	0.78	1400	1.37	1426	1.36	2074	1.91	1663	1.48
Yellow fever	5	0.01			374	0.36	599	0.55	1531	1.36
Measles	1431	1.45	1721	1.69	1991	1.89	1369	1.26	968	0.86
Pneumonia	530	0.54	873	0.86	524	0.50	534	0.49	709	0.63
Dysentery	202	0.20	422	0.41	339	0.32	424	0.39	599	0.53
Meningitis	82	0.08	96	0.09	1469	1.40	1546	1.42	496	0.44
Tuberculosis	161	0.16	354	0.35	515	0.49	422	0.39	423	0.38
Tetanus	209	0.21	219	0.21	157	0.15	142	0.13	334	0.30

Source: Department of Planning, Research and Statistics, Federal Ministry of Health, Lagos 1990.

prevalent in recent years. Reported measles cases rose 76 per cent between 1984 and 1985 alone, from 122,591 to 161,768, and cases of whooping cough reported during the same years rose 68 per cent, from 62,751 to 92,266.

Mortality figures for certain diseases also suggest the adverse impact of structural adjustment: cholera, another water-borne disease, took 136 lives between 1979 and 1983 but accounted for 325 deaths between 1984 and 1988. This rapid rise in mortality can be attributed to deteriorating sanitation, water quality, and food quality. Measles, a treatable disease to the extent health services are adequate, resulted in 7480 deaths between 1984 and 1988. While only five deaths were reported in 1984 from yellow fever, another treatable ailment, the mortality figures shot up subsequently to 374 in 1986, 599 in 1987, and 1531 in 1988. Tuberculosis and pneumonia, which owing to proper and prompt diagnosis and treatment were on the decline in Nigeria before structural adjustment, claimed 1875 and 3179 lives respectively in 1984–8.

Anecdotal evidence suggests further negative effects of structural adjustment on health. For example, the incidence of kwashiorkor was not nearly so acute in the 1970s as it is today. Cases are now evident on city streets, and many children brought to clinics for treatment of minor ailments exhibit symptoms of kwashiorkor as well. A 1988–9 study found stunted growth among 51 per cent of two-year-old children in Lagos and its rural hinterlands, and Lagos is considerably more affluent than most areas of the country.

Malnutrition is such that it is not unusual to observe both adults and children struggling for food remnants at public functions. Nor is it uncommon to see human scavengers roaming from one waste dump to another in search of food: such behaviour was the exclusive preserve of lunatics in the 1970s yet today is common to all hungry people. Both children and able-bodied, supposedly educated adults can be seen begging for their sustenance. Destitute persons sleep under bridges, by the roadside, and in any open space. Such an existence of course has negative effects on well-being, and these persons have no access to health services.

Conclusions and Recommendations

In conclusion, it is clear that the net effect of structural adjustment has been negative with regard to health and health care for Nigerians. It has resulted in increased prevalence of disease, malnutrition, and lowered resistance to infection. While successive governments have advocated the provision of free health care, the cost of care has actually increased under structural adjustment. Indeed, it appears that the government has abandoned not only the notion of free health care but of 'health' itself for its nationals. The scenario has been one of greater propaganda and less funding. While the slogan 'Health for all by the year 2000' has been widely publicized, popular ingenuity has produced the more accurate parody, 'Hell for all by the year 2000.'

Moreover, such a negative characterization of structural adjustment's consequences is borne out by the actions taken by those most affected. Rioting initiated by students in May 1989 demanded the restoration not only of free education but also of free health services. The protests rapidly spread beyond students to involve wide sectors of the urban poor, schoolchildren, and artisans.

Despite the markedly negative consequences of the actual structural adjustment programme implemented, it is appropriate to point out that some adjustment of the economy is required. At best, however, the current programme merely changes the mode of operation of the economy while leaving its operators intact to continue to milk it to their own benefit and to the detriment of the bulk of the population. Structural adjustment has yet to structurally change the economy, and rather has had adverse effects on the life, health, and welfare of the people without giving them much to show for their hardships.

To redress some of these balances and effect a more just distribution of the pains and benefits of structural adjustment, ameliorative measures will have to be adopted and the current free fall of the economy arrested. Measures that have had unforeseen consequences will need to be reversed. For example, removal of fuel subsidies and the resulting rise in transportation costs has rendered the prices of foodstuffs brought from remote rural areas to the cities nearly prohibitive.

With regard to health care, it is clear that this sector needs to be adequately funded, with attention devoted above all to developing the Primary Health Scheme that could bring services within the reach of the poor and rural dwellers. Drugs need to be made available at affordable prices. To achieve the latter aim, government must rationalize the allocation of foreign exchange and monitor the types of drugs imported, ensuring that the essential ones are given priority. In addition, agriculture should be accorded high priority in the allocation of foreign exchange. Agro-based industries need protection from foreign competition and subsidies if adequate and affordable food supplies are to be achieved. An annual immunization programme should be launched to reduce the frequency of outbreaks of childhood diseases. Indeed, such immunization should be made mandatory for admittance to primary schools. Balanced diets for schoolchildren should also be subsidized to reduce the prevalence of malnutrition.

Structural adjustment should be transformed into corrective measures to restructure the economy as a whole, rather than emphasizing fiscal measures alone. Real gains from structural adjustment, such as those from the sale of foreign exchange, should be dedicated to improving the welfare of those whose living standards have fallen below the absolute minimum for survival as a consequence of the programme.

Finally, there is no doubt that structural adjustment has introduced far-reaching changes into the nation's economic life. It has evoked adaptive strategies on the part of the people and thereby rekindled a sense of creativity and ingenuity on the part of many. This has had both negative and positive consequences. To the extent that local manufactures have arisen to reduce the pain inflicted by structural adjustment, it has been positive. Yet to the extent that fraudulent practices, embezzlement, misappropriation of funds, and even drug trafficking have multiplied, such 'creativity' has been negative.

A critical reappraisal of structural adjustment is needed so as to improve living standards and address the imbalances in the distribution of structural adjustment's gains and pains. Some economic restructuring is needed, but a more humane policy will gain greater support among the people. For the poor, the unemployed, or the retrenched worker, structural adjustment has thus far produced but further impoverishment, deteriorating health, malnutrition, and stress.

9 Nigeria
Consequences for Education

T. O. Fadayomi

Introduction

The education sector has always been given high priority in Nigeria's development efforts. After the establishment of constitutional rule in 1951, which gave the federal and regional governments concurrent responsibility for educational policy, the Western Region inaugurated in 1955 the first system of free, universal primary education. This brought the creation of large numbers of primary schools, the expansion of existing secondary schools, and the construction of additional, modern secondary institutions. The latter stressed practical education in a three-year programme. Recurrent spending on education by the Western Regional government amounted to between 30.7 per cent and 39.9 per cent of the total budget during the 1953–8 period (Taiwo, 1980).

A parallel expansion of education was projected in the Eastern Region, where free, universal primary education during the first four years was offered on the condition that local authorities would pay 45 per cent of the costs. This more modest scheme was owing to the difficult financial situation of the region at the time. The scheme could not be fully implemented, and only the first two years of primary schooling were eventually made free.

Education was already virtually free in the Northern Region, inasmuch as fees were quite low in both the government and the native authority schools, and anyone who could not pay was exempted from fees. The policy was effectively the same in the voluntary agency schools. However, many local authorities in the north were apathetic toward western-style education and believed that it served to corrupt the student (Taiwo, 1980). Even so, some expansion did occur, though the numbers did not reflect the size of the region. New primary schools were established and middle schools were upgraded to full secondary schools. Teacher training institutions were reorganized and upgraded.

Lagos was initially included in the Western Region scheme, but, after the 1954 constitution established the Federal Territory of Lagos, education there became the responsibility of the Federal Ministry of Education and the Lagos City Council. Free universal eight-year primary education was instituted in Lagos in 1957.

Despite the differences in timing and problems of finance and management in certain regions, educational expansion continued through the 1960s. Primary school enrolment reached 30 per cent for the nation as a whole in 1966; the ratio was only 3 per cent at the secondary level, however. Moreover, serious imbalances in development persisted among different regions of the country, with primary enrolment ranging from a mere 4 per cent in some areas to a high 70 per cent in others. At the secondary level, the range was between 0.4 per cent and 12 per cent.

High drop-out rates in primary schools after the onset of free education schemes have been attributed to inadequate facilities and poor quality of teaching. Likewise, failure to achieve a comparable expansion of secondary education resulted in serious unemployment among school leavers. Shortages of teaching staff were recorded throughout the period despite efforts to expand teachers' training facilities.

Under the Second and Third National Development Plans between 1970 and 1980, policy shifted toward a more functional approach and education was regarded as a powerful instrument for social change and nation-building. Efforts were geared to expanding facilities, reforming content, and strengthening the machinery of educational development. Universal free primary education (UPE) was launched in 1976 and was to be made compulsory in 1979. Government policy also called for expanding secondary education to permit the fullest possible enrolment of primary-school leavers as well as to ensure adequate input for expanded tertiary and higher education levels (Nigeria, 1975). With the return to civilian rule in 1979, some states that had already had considerable success with universal primary education since 1955 now initiated universal secondary education within their territories (these included the states of Lagos, Bendel, Ogun, Ondo, and Oyo).

Impact of Structural Adjustment

As Nigeria's economic resources dwindled after 1982, and especially after the onset of severe balance of payments problems in 1985, it became increasingly difficult for the government to meet the financial needs of all sectors of the economy. Not least affected was the education sector, which during the period of the oil boom had witnessed massive expansion of student population and infrastructural facilities. Enrolment of primary-school pupils had doubled in 1975–80, rising from slightly over 6 million to more than 12 million. Secondary-school enrolment had risen still faster, from about 0.6 million in 1975 to 1.5 million in 1980. Rapid increases had likewise been registered in tertiary institutions such as the Colleges of Education, the Colleges of Technology, and the University.

These trends were reversed in the 1980s. While primary-school enrolment had reached 90 per cent in 1980, it declined steadily to 64 per cent in 1987. The transition rate from primary to post-primary institutions dropped from 67 per cent in 1979 to 47 per cent in 1984. While recurrent expenditures continued to rise until 1985 (from an average of 6.5 per cent of budget before 1980 to 10.7 per cent in 1980—5), these declined subsequently to an average 6.9 per cent of budget in 1986–9. Capital spending on education as percentage of budget declined from 9.7 per cent up to 1979, to 4.4 per cent in 1980–5, to 3.1 per cent in 1986–9. Total educational spending by the

Federal Government of Nigeria dropped from 16.2 per cent of budget through 1979 to only 10 per cent of budget in 1986–9.

This deterioration in enrolment and spending on education can be attributed directly to the worsening economic situation. In an attempt to offset the effects of federal budget cuts, cost-recovery measures were introduced by the various state governments. These contributed further to the enrolment decline as education costs became unbearable for families that were suffering from retrenchment and/or substantial reduction in real incomes. The quality of education has also declined, as the supply of qualified teachers has fallen short of demand, physical facilities have been allowed to deteriorate, and necessary teaching materials have been lacking.

Within this framework, certain counter-measures have been taken. The federal government now helps to fund primary education, whereas before it was solely the responsibility of the state and local governments. To make secondary education more functional and practically oriented, a two-tier system has been introduced so that recipients receive some employable skills. Textbooks and other pertinent materials have begun to be subsidized.

While the government battles to improve the overall quality of education, both drop-outs and unemployed graduates from the formal educational system increasingly find means of acquiring skills and training in the informal sector of the nation's economy. This sector encompasses a wide range of activities involving processing, repairs, and services – such as hairdressing, butchery, battery charging, vulcanizing, carpentry, mechanics, blacksmithing, brickmaking, and trading (Fadayomi et al., 1989). Most of the training acquired therein is through apprenticeships. Operators and entrepreneurs in the informal sector trades are the major sources of skills dissemination to newly recruited apprentices. Masters instruct the recruits directly and indirectly in a hierarchical structure. The apprentice learns production management, sales skills, and costing directly from the master, or else the master passes instruction down indirectly from the oldest journeyman or apprentice to the youngest. Since there are no organized classes within this informal system, apprentices with some schooling pass their formal knowledge on to others. So in this system apprentices learn in both vertical and horizontal fashion, both from the masters and from their colleagues.

Some of the current programmes adopted as a consequence of the economic malaise in the country aim at stimulating self-employment and derive from the recognition that informal sector activities should be developed in order to enhance employment opportunities and the overall standard of living. The National Directorate of Employment has been charged with the responsibility for job creation in the informal sector. It has initiated the National Employment and Vocational Skill Development Programme, which includes:

- the national open apprenticeship scheme, which provides unemployed youth with basic skills needed in the economy;
- the Waste-to-Wealth scheme, aimed at encouraging conversion of neglected waste materials and scraps into useful products;
- the Schools-on-Wheels scheme, which seeks to stem rampant rural-to-urban migration by introducing fully-equipped mobile vocational training facilities into rural areas; and

- a disabled work scheme that provides self-employment to the disabled with the aid of special facilities that enable them to acquire appropriate skills and training.

Summary and Recommendations

As have many other African governments, Nigeria has had to effect substantial cuts in public social expenditures in order to reduce budget deficits and release resources for debt service (Ninsin, 1990). The Nigerian education system has consequently faced inadequate facilities and funding, declining enrolment rates, and an overall decline in educational quality.

The public response – mitigated by the economic crisis – has involved efforts to boost financial support for primary education, reorient secondary schools to stress the acquisition of practical skills, and find ways to subsidize textbooks and other pertinent materials.

In the current situation, many families are unable to pay the fees entailed by the cost-recovery measures adopted by the various state governments. Hence drop-outs, early school leavers, and unemployed graduates of formal institutions are seeking more employable skills in the informal-sector trades. Given the additional government support to such schemes, the informal sector has burgeoned in recent times.

The economic adjustment programme is oriented toward a 'return to the free market'; hence policies are designed to strengthen the private sector and liberalize trade based on the capitalist notion of the efficiency of market forces. As a consequence, subsidies for public sector enterprises, and for social services above all, are being withdrawn (Ninsin, 1990). In effect, the government is dismantling some of its institutions that serve the critical needs of society in exchange for a policy of making the economy safe and profitable for private capital both local and foreign. It is to be hoped that the government at the same time will adopt appropriate fiscal policies so as to release sufficient revenue for critical social services such as education.

Table 9.1. Nigeria, trends in student and teacher population in the formal schooling system, 1975–1980

| | Primary | | Secondary | | Technical/Vocational | | Tertiary (students) | | Universities |
	Teachers	Pupils	Teachers	Pupils	Teachers	Pupils	College of Education	College of Technology	(students)
1975–1976	177,221	6,165,547	7148	601,652	4769	27,834			32,286
1976–1977	251,362	8,100,324	12,282	730,899	5832	29,858	7793		31,110
1977–1978	291,457	9,867,961	15,031	913,648	7206	40,538	13,768	17,411	37,558
1978–1979	301,427	10,798,550	19,993	1,194,479	7318	46,712	16,792	23,021	49,423
1979–1980	343,551	12,117,483	26,261	1,553,345	7380	61,856	26,300	30,470	57,502

Source: Federal Ministry of Education, Statistics of Education in Nigeria 1980–1984, Lagos, 1985.

Table 9.2. Nigeria, primary and secondary enrolment, 1980–1988

	Primary		Secondary	
	Total Enrolled	% Change	Total Enrolled	% Change
1980–1981	13,777,642		1,990,550	
1981–1982	14,325,166	3.97	2,503,671	25.77
1982–1983	14,641,799	2.21	2,873,937	14.79
1983–1984	14,300,501	–2.33	2,181,067	–24.11
1984–1985	13,025,287	–8.91	2,596,586	19.05
1985–1986	11,527,974	–11.49	2,128,364	–18.03
1986–1987	11,275,270	–2.19	2,843,681	33.61
1987–1988	12,225,337	8.40	2,934,469	3.19

Source: Federal Ministry of Education, Statistics Section, Lagos, August 1988.

Table 9.3. Nigeria, enrolment ratios in primary and secondary education, 1980–1987

Year	Primary, % enrolled (population 6–11 years)	Secondary, % enrolled (population 12–17 years)
1980–1981	91	18.94
1981–1982	93	22.52
1982–1983	93	24.49
1983–1984	88	22.55
1984–1985	78.1	
1985–1986	75.5	
1986–1987	64.3	

Source: Federal Republic of Nigeria, Situation of Children and Women in Nigeria (UNICEF, August 1989); Federal Ministry of Education, *Statistics of Education in Nigeria 1980–1984*, Lagos, 1985.

Table 9.4. Nigeria, transition rates from primary to post-primary institutions, 1979–1984

Year	Transition rate
1979–80 to 1980–81	66.92
1980–81 to 1981–82	61.68
1981–82 to 1982–83	53.69
1982–83 to 1983–84	46.49

Source: Federal Ministry of Education, *Statistics of Education in Nigeria 1980–1984*, Lagos, 1985.

Table 9.5. Nigeria, recurrent and capital expenditures on education by the Federal Government, 1975–89

	(in millions of current Naira)			(as % of total budget)		
Year	Recurrent	Capital	Total education	Recurrent	Capital	Total education
1975	218.9	631.1	850.00	4.6	17.9	22.50
1976	522.0	529.2	1051.20	9.6	12.5	22.10
1977	236.8	500.0	736.80	3.1	6.5	9.60
1978	268.2	301.4	569.60	3.9	5.3	9.20
1979	360.4	306.7	667.10	11.3	6.3	17.60
1980	509.1	729.4	1238.50	8.5	8.7	17.20
1981	712.8	217.2	930.00	14.0	3.8	17.80
1982	541.3	402.8	944.10	9.8	5.8	15.60
1983	620.8	346.6	967.40	11.8	5.1	16.90
1984	675.9	87.6	763.50	10.5	1.6	12.10
1985	697.2	126.2	823.40	9.7	1.5	11.20
1986	483.8	391.4	875.20	6.3	4.3	10.60
1987	354.0	94.6	448.60	2.3	1.5	3.80
1988	1458.8	327.9	1786.70	7.5	3.9	11.40
1989	3011.8	387.2	3399.00	11.6	2.6	14.20

Note: Data for 1979, 1980, and 1984–6 are actual expenditures; data for 1975–8, 1981, 1982, and 1987–9 are provisional estimates; data for 1983 are approved estimates.
Source: Central Bank of Nigeria, Annual Report and Statement of Accounts, 1975–89.

References

Central Bank of Nigeria (1987). *Annual Report and Statement of Accounts*. Lagos: Central Bank of Nigeria.

Paul Collier (1983). 'Oil and Inequality in Rural Nigeria'. In Dharam Ghai and Samir Radwan, eds, *Agrarian Policies and Rural Development in Africa*. Geneva: International Labour Organization.

T. O. Fadayomi (1988). *Social Development Strategies, Policies and Programmes in West Africa in the Light of the Lagos Plan of Action: Case Studies of Ghana, Nigeria and Gambia*. Tripoli: ACARTSOD.

T. O. Fadayomi *et al.* (1989). *Education and Training for Skills and Income in the Urban Informal Sector in Sub-Saharan Africa: The Case of Urban Informal Sector of Ibadan City, Nigeria*. World Bank/NISER.

Federal Ministry of Budget and Planning (1990). *First National Rolling Plan, 1990–2*. Lagos.

National Directorate of Employment (n.d.). *Creating More Job Opportunities*. Lagos.

Nigeria, Second National Development Plan, 1970–4 (1970). Lagos: Federal Ministry of Information.

Nigeria, Third National Development Plan, 1975–80 (1975). Lagos: Central Planning Office, Federal Ministry of Economic Development.

Kwame Ninsin (1990). 'Ghana Under the PNDC: Delinking or Structural Adjustment?'. In Azzan Mah-Jorib, ed., *Adjustment or Delinking: The African Experience*. United Nations University Press.

F. A. Olaloku *et al.* (1979). *Structure of the Nigerian Economy*. Lagos: The Macmillan Press and the University of Lagos Press.

Olatunde Oloko (1979). 'Report on Modernization and Socio-Political Problems in Africa'. Lagos, unpublished manuscript.

A. Osoba (1989). 'The Development of the Informal Sector During the Period of the Structural Adjustment Programme in Nigeria'. In *Small Scale Industry and the Informal Sector and Training in Sub-Saharan Africa*. Ibadan: Nigerian Institute of Social and Economic Research.

C. O. Taiwo (1980). *The Nigerian Educational System: Past, Present and Future*. Lagos: Thomas Nelson.

Duru Tobi *et al.* (1987). 'Sacrifice and Pain as Inevitable Costs of Adjustment'. In A. O. Phillips and E. C. Ndekwu, eds, *Structural Adjustment Programme in a Developing Economy: The Case of Nigeria*. Ibadan: University of Ibadan Press.

10 Malawi

C. Chipeta

A Profile of the Economy

Output and employment

Malawi's total land area is 118,000 square kilometres, of which 94,000 is land and the rest water. Preliminary figures from the 1987 census put the population at 7.9 million. Population growth is estimated at 3.5 per cent per annum, and the population has doubled during the quarter century since independence in 1964. The population density of 85 persons per square kilometre is among the highest in Africa, exceeded perhaps only by Burundi and Rwanda (World Bank, 1990). Per capita Gross National Product is said to have amounted to US$160 per capita in 1987, making Malawi one of the five poorest countries on earth, despite a 60 per cent increase since 1964* (World Bank, 1989).

Malawi's post-independence economy can be divided into two broad phases. Before 1979, rapid growth occurred in many sectors (though the economy was sluggish in 1964–9). Since 1979, decline in growth rates has been succeeded by uneven recovery. In the earlier phase, annual increases in Gross Domestic Product averaged 6.1 per cent, with per capita income growing an average of 2.5 per cent per annum. Rising output was particularly marked in agriculture and in import-substitution manufacturing based on imported inputs. Rising domestic demand for consumer and intermediate goods stimulated production, as did increased export demand. This phase also witnessed the building of infrastructure, especially in the transport and utility sectors.

Economic growth before 1979 stimulated government revenue, which increased at an annual rate of 16 per cent. Spending rose in line with GDP, averaging about 25 per cent thereof. The overall deficit, though mounting, remained moderate and averaged about 8 per cent of GDP. Much of the deficit was financed by concessionary official

---

* These figures must be treated with considerable caution, in that the reliability of national income estimates is quite low. Value-added data for the government sector are believed to be generally reliable, those for large private enterprises fairly so, and those for the 'other' category – which includes 'own-account' or subsistence – are reliable to order-of-magnitude only (National Statistics Office, 1968). The problem with the latter lies in improper demarcation of the production boundary, in estimating production volumes, and in valuing output itself. Value-added in this sector is thus believed to be a gross underestimation.

capital inflows and by domestic resources. The net contribution from foreign official sources between 1964 and 1978 ranged between 70 and 85 per cent (Malawi Government, 1983: 16). Resort to the domestic banking system was modest during this period; domestic borrowing financed some 15 to 20 per cent of the overall deficit and constituted about 2 per cent of GDP.

Capital formation accelerated as well, with gross domestic investment (GDI) growing at a 20 per cent average annual rate to reach 28 per cent of GDP in 1980. Government investment rose more rapidly than did private, with its contribution reaching 32 per cent of GDI by 1980. This was made possible by resource mobilization. At independence, domestic savings were negligible and virtually all capital expenditures were financed from abroad. Before 1969 gross national savings financed only 8 per cent of investment, but by 1979 this figure had risen to 50 per cent. Private savings reached 90 per cent of private sector investment in 1979. Government recurrent expenditures were restrained, and surpluses in 1972–3 helped finance part of the development programme. As domestic savings increased, the share of foreign financing in total investment fell from 92 per cent in 1967 to 50 per cent in 1979. Inflation remained moderate, averaging 6.5 per cent per annum in 1965–75. This reflected favourable supplies of goods and modest domestic pressures.

Exports tripled in value between 1967 and 1975, owing mainly to expanding agricultural production. However, industrialization and infrastructure projects meant that imports increased still faster. While the ratio of the merchandise trade deficit to GDP rose, the trend was moderated by generally favourable net barter terms of trade. These deficits were typically financed by short- and long-term capital inflows as the government's development programme received support from both bilateral donors and international agencies. The overall balance of payments was in surplus in seven of the eleven years from 1965 to 1975.

Less satisfactory performance has been registered by Malawi's economy since 1978. Real GDP growth fell to 0.4 per cent in 1980 and –5.2 per cent in 1981, then reached 2.8 per cent in 1982 and 4.1 per cent in both 1983 and 1984 – all well below the growth rates registered in the earlier period. This deceleration can be attributed to adverse weather conditions, low incentives provided to farmers, rising costs, untimely delivery of imported inputs owing to disruption of traditional overland routes to seaports, and the overall weakening in the world economy, which meant a deterioration in the country's terms of trade. The initial recovery in the mid-1980s was due to the return of normal weather, the strengthening of producer incentives, and the rerouting of trade to alternate routes (Malawi Government, 1983: 16).

Decline resumed in 1986, with real GDP growing at only 2.8 per cent that year and declining by 1.5 per cent the next. The decline was due largely to factors beyond Malawi's control: a fall in the world market price of tea, deterioration in the net barter terms of trade, a refugee burden, and continued external transport problems (Malawi Government, 1988). Improved availability of imported inputs facilitated renewed GDP growth of 3.6 per cent in 1988 (Malawi Government, 1989).

Growth of government tax revenues slowed as a consequence of the recession (total revenues and grants fell from 24.3 per cent of GDP in 1979–80 to 19.9 per cent in 1980–1). At the same time, government expenditures rose sharply (from 24 per cent of GDP in 1977–8 to 34 per cent in 1980–1) to meet higher foreign debt obligations and large development outlays, to finance maize and fuel imports, and to cover operating shortfalls of statutory bodies. The overall deficit accelerated from 6.2 per cent of GDP in 1977–8 to 11 per cent in 1980–1. Fiscal deficits were accompanied by an increase in domestic bank borrowing, with a markedly expansionary impact on aggregate demand. Foreign commercial borrowing was also required, raising not only the level of foreign debt but also the debt-service ratio (as borrowing came at higher interest rates), from 11.3 per cent in 1977–8 to 44 per cent in 1982.

Meanwhile, domestic savings fell, initially from 14.9 per cent of GDP in 1979 to 11.4 per cent in 1980. While government development expenditures continued to mount, the overall investment rate fell from 34 per cent of GDP in 1979 to 21 per cent in 1981. By 1986, the domestic savings rate had declined to 9.2 per cent and the investment rate to 11.1 per cent.

Inflationary conditions in the world economy, external transport difficulties, and unsatisfactory agricultural output also quickened the pace of increase in consumer prices, which averaged 10 per cent from 1975 through 1984 and became persistently high after that. Foreign exchange shortages, sporadic droughts, deficit financing, and rising import costs due to transport difficulties and currency devaluations have all contributed.

Droughts reduced agricultural production and export volumes, while the worldwide recession weakened demand. Export prices, especially those for Malawi's principal exports of tobacco and tea, declined by an average of 40 per cent while the costs of fuel and other essential imports such as fertilizer and capital goods escalated. The import bill for petroleum products alone more than doubled between 1978 and 1981, despite a decline in import volume. Use of alternative, longer transport routes cost more than did the railway through Mozambique, and this too contributed to the higher import bills.

Consequently, the net barter terms of trade deteriorated by 30 per cent while the current accounts deficit rose sharply from 7 per cent of GDP in 1977 to 18 per cent in 1980. Capital inflows rose only modestly and did not fully cover the current account deficits. Gross foreign reserves fell from the equivalent of five months of imports in 1977 to less than two months in 1981. The net foreign assets of the banking system became consistently negative. Eventually, Malawi had to reschedule its debt payments through Paris and London Club negotiations, obtaining relief equal to some K124.5 million in 1982–4. The overall balance of payments deficit reached K109.7 million in 1986, owing largely to mounting foreign debt obligations. After further postponement of some debt payments, a surplus of K85.5 million was registered in 1987 (Malawi Government, 1988). Additional rescheduling led to a larger surplus of K247.2 million in 1988 (Malawi Government, 1989).

Formal-sector wage employment in Malawi grew rapidly between 1968 and 1988 (8.3 per cent per annum), owing to the high rate of output expansion (World Bank, 1981). Some 16,100 new jobs were created every year, on average. But since the labour force grew by about 66,400 workers annually, the remaining 50,300 had to be absorbed by the smallholder sector, the informal sector, and migration abroad, or else enter the ranks of the unemployed. Sluggish growth in the 1980s has meant that formal-sector employment has now been rising by only 4 per cent a year. Thus some 60,000 new entrants to the labour force annually cannot be absorbed.

Table 10.1.   Malawi, selected macro-economic indicators, 1965–1989

	1965	1979	1980	1981	1982	1983	1984	1985	1986	1987	1988	1989	Proj.
Population (millions)		5.9	6.4	6.2	6.4	6.6	6.4	7.1	7.3	7.5	7.7	8.2	
Population growth rate, %		3.1	3.1	3.1	3.1	3.2	3.2	3.2	3.2	3.2	3.2	3.5	
Change in real GDP,%		5.5	-0.4	-5.2	2.8	4.1	4.5	4.2	2.8	1.5	3.6	4.3	4.1
Change in													
consumption, %			19.6	10.1	8.2	14.7	23.5	16.5	17.5	20.2	40.0	23.9	
Government, %			13.5	2.7	9.9	6.3	14.2	28.4	26.1	13.2	2.2	11.5	
Private, %			21.2	13.3	7.7	17.1	25.8	13.3	15.3	22.2	49.6	26.0	
Stock building, %			-100.6	7.4	206.5	60.8	-61.5	104.9	-94.5	828.3	136.8	-23.1	
Change in domestic saving, %			12.5	20.9	42.2	23.8	23.8	1.4	-21.4	60.2	-40.3	-11.7	
Formal sector													
employment (thousands)			352	367	327	344	387	381	411	407	429		
Change, %			4.3	-10.9	5.2	12.5	-1.6	7.6	4.1	-4.9	5.4		
Inflation rate, %			11.0	18.3	9.6	9.4	15.4	11.0	15.1	15.0	26.7	31.5	10.0
Primary school enrolment													
ratio	44	59			62	63	62	62					
Secondary school enrolment													
ratio	2	4	4	4	4	5	4	4					
Higher education enrolment													
ratio	1	1	1	1	1	1	1	1					
Life expectancy at birth	40		44	44	44	44	45	45	45	46			
Infant mortality rate	199		172			164	158	156	153	153			
Child death rate	55		39			38	38	35					

Source: Malawi Government, Economic Reports (various), Lilongwe: Department of Economic Planning and Development; and World Bank, World Development Reports (various), New York: Oxford University Press.

Table 10.2. Malawi, literacy rates, 1964–1986

Year	%
1964[*]	10
1977	18
1985[**]	41
1986[***]	45

Source: Nyirenda and Moyo, 1990.
[*]   See Statement of Development Policies 1987–1996, p. 127.
[**] See World Bank, Education in Sub-Saharan Africa: Policies for Adjustment, Revitalization and Expansion, 1988, p. 168.
[***] Calculated from 1987 Census, Preliminary Results

Table 10.3. Malawi, primary school pupil/teacher ratios, by district, 1981–1982

Region	District	Pupil/Teacher Ratio
NORTHERN	Chitipa	59:1
	Karonga	52:1
	Nkhata Bay	56:1
	Rumphi	48:1
	Mzimba	61:1
CENTRAL	Kasungu	67:1
	Nkhota-Kota	61:1
	Ntchisi	45:1
	Dowa	65:1
	Salima	61:1
	Lilongwe	50:1 Urban
		66:1 Rural
	Mchinji	57:1
	Dedza	65:1
	Ntcheu	93:1
SOUTHERN	Mangochi	60:1
	Zomba	50:1 Urban only
	Chiradzulu	74:1
	Blantyre	61:1 Urban
		74:1 Rural
	Mwanza	46:1
	Thyolo	70:1
	Mulanje	95:1
	Chikwawa	65:1
	Nsanje	49:1

Source: Ministry of Education, Education Statistics 1983. Lilongwe: Ministry of Education.

Education

Until recently, education in Malawi has been viewed as a catalyst for development, that is, as a means of providing skilled personnel for employment in the high-priority agriculture sector and elsewhere. It was hoped that domestic training of skilled personnel would reduce dependence on expatriates and facilitate more rapid economic growth by removing the skilled personnel constraint. It has now been recognized, however, that because of limited paid-employment opportunities education must be geared more toward training for self-employment. Still, lack of compulsory universal education and resource limitations have yielded only slow progress toward that goal. The gross primary enrolment ratio, for example, increased from 44 per cent in 1965 to only 62 per cent in 1982 (for males, from 55 per cent to 75 per cent; for females, from 32 per cent to 51 per cent). The secondary enrolment ratio increased from 2 per cent in 1965 to 4 per cent in 1982, and in university education the ratio reached 1 per cent only in 1984. Substantial gains have been made in attaining adult literacy, however. (See Tables 10.1–10.3.)

Inasmuch as there is an inverse relationship between education for women and family size, the smaller proportion of female enrolment is cause for concern. Providing more education to women would reduce fertility by raising the opportunity cost of time spent in childbearing, provided, of course, that formal-sector employment was available. In fact, resources devoted to creating such employment opportunities are more influential than educating women *per se*. Additional benefits would accrue from greater stress on women's education, however, such as a reduction in the earnings gap between men and women. More women would no doubt migrate to urban areas seeking formal-sector employment, and some might engage in international migration. These things would also assist in altering attitudes toward childbearing and thus reduce average family size.

Education policy currently aims at developing an efficient and high-quality system appropriate to the country's available resources and to the economic and social aspirations of its population. Low quality and inefficiency in the educational system are attributable in part to the large pupil–teacher ratios (Table 10.3); these limit individual attention and the amount of class and home work teachers can attend to. The relative scarcity of classrooms and teachers rules out all-day attendance. Further problems are caused by inadequate supplies, supervision, facilities, and personnel. Some of these might be minimized through greater private-enterprise involvement in the education system. Others can be solved through curriculum reform and improved management.

Further aims of education policy involve promoting national consciousness and cohesion, but just how the system will attain these has not been stated. Nor is it clear how education will contribute to reinforcing the country's high ethical standards, something that is essential if fairness is to be maintained amidst rapid economic progress. In promoting national consciousness, emphasis will probably be placed on the study of national history and civics. As to national cohesion, the study of religion (Islam, Christianity, traditional African religions) may possibly be the salvation. At present, though, religion in school is synonymous with Bible study, despite the fact that most students are non-Christians. Social studies could also play a role, although current courses in civics have little to do with the lives of ordinary people or with African culture, which is rich in safeguards for economic equality.

Table 10.4. Malawi, sectoral expenditures as per cent of total revenue account expenditures, 1978–1989 (for fiscal years beginning in year stated)

	1978	1979	1980	1981	1982	1983	1984	1985	1986	1987	1988*
General services	36.0	32.6	28.7	25.8	30.0	30.1	24.2	27.6	23.9	24.0	26.0
Administration	13.7	13.1	11.7	9.3	13.4	16.0	10.4	12.9	9.4	11.1	15.0
Defence	13.7	10.1	8.7	8.2	6.8	7.1	6.5	9.4	7.5	6.5	5.8
Justice	8.6	9.4	8.4	8.3	9.7	6.9	7.3	7.3	7.0	6.3	5.2
Social services	23.2	21.3	21.3	19.7	18.9	19.8	18.1	16.9	18.9	17.3	16.8
Education	12.7	11.8	11.4	10.1	11.3	11.3	9.6	8.9	9.1	9.6	9.1
Health	7.4	7.0	7.2	6.9	6.3	6.9	6.7	7.5	7.2	5.6	5.5
Community and social	3.2	2.5	2.7	2.8	1.3	1.7	1.8	0.5	2.4	2.2	2.2
Economic services	13.3	12.9	12.0	11.8	14.7	14.4	11.9	14.8	14.1	13.6	12.7
Unallocable services	27.5	33.2	38.0	42.8	36.5	35.7	45.8	40.7	43.1	45.1	44.5
Public debt	14.4	21.2	27.2	34.1	27.9	26.0	37.8	36.0	37.9	40.2	39.0
Pensions and gratuities	2.1	2.1	1.2	1.5	1.7	1.5	1.1	1.2	1.1	1.5	1.5
Other	11.0	9.9	9.6	7.2	6.9	8.2	6.9	3.5	4.1	3.4	4.0

* Estimates.
Source: Nyirenda and Moyo, 1990.

Health care

The principal diseases afflicting people in Malawi are, in order of incidence, malaria, nutritional deficiencies, respiratory infections, ailments affecting the abdomen and gastro-intestinal tract, skin conditions, other diarrheal diseases, inflammatory eye diseases, and traumatic conditions. The number of AIDS cases is substantial. Access to health care is both inadequate and unevenly distributed, although there has been improvement in certain respects since independence. Ratios of population to care providers have been substantially reduced: there were 46,900 persons per physician in 1965, but only 11,560 in 1984. The number of persons per nurse stood at 12,670 in 1965 but came down to 3130 in 1984. Life expectancy at birth has increased from 40 years in 1965 to 46 today, and the infant and child mortality rates have declined significantly (Table 10.1).

The distribution of medical facilities by district is badly skewed; however, inasmuch as major hospitals are used as referrals by many districts and all regions, the effective distribution is rather more even than the data imply. To a large extent the maldistribution of health centres reflects a government policy of distributing public service facilities evenly among districts without regard to the population thereof.

Health-care delivery is inadequate because its development has received low priority, especially in the past. Ratios of recurrent expenditures on health services were low in the 1970s and show little sign of improvement. The share of health in the current budget declined from 5.5 per cent in 1972 to 5.2 per cent in 1982. While efforts are still constrained by budgetary resources, there is growing awareness that progress in other sectors can be achieved rapidly only if health services are more fully developed. For this reason, development policy for the 1980s placed greater emphasis on health care than was the case in the previous decade.

Stabilization and Structural Adjustment

Introduction

Malawi since 1979 has implemented a series of stabilization programmes under the auspices of the International Monetary Fund and structural adjustment programmes supported first by the World Bank and later by both the Bank and the IMF. All these programmes have been designed to respond to problems of external and internal financial imbalances, low rates of economic growth, and inflation. While stabilization measures have aimed at short- or medium-term improvements in fiscal and monetary management, structural adjustment measures have had long-term goals and have gone beyond financial policies to encompass institutional reforms. The various programmes are reviewed briefly in the following section before proceeding to an examination of their consequences.

The first stabilization programme was initiated in August 1979. It was to have lasted two and a half years but was abandoned in 1980 owing to unforeseen deterioration of the terms of trade, unfavourable weather conditions, and disruption of land routes through Mozambique. Ceilings on bank credit expansion were not observed as a result. A new two-year standby arrangement went into effect in 1980; performance thereunder was mixed, and the overall balance of payments remained with a sizeable deficit. A holding operation followed in August 1982, when Malawi entered a one-year standby arrangement with the IMF as the first part of a medium-term adjustment programme (IMF, 1983: 322). The country achieved some measure of financial stability and restrained domestic demand. The extended arrangement was completed in 1986 after slippages on credit ceilings had led to a suspension of drawings. The new accord went into effect in early 1988, as a precondition for external debt-service rescheduling (IMF, 1988a: 71). Soon thereafter, Malawi entered into an enhanced structural adjustment agreement (IMF, 1988b: 252–3).

Structural adjustment had been initiated earlier, in 1981–3, with the following aims: restoring the real growth rate to 4.8 per cent (2 per cent per capita); diversifying sources of foreign exchange through promotion of new crops and agro-industries and the revival of smallholder-produced crops; raising smallholder producer prices; and reducing external and internal financial imbalances. The government agreed to raise tariffs charged to various parastate enterprises and to review exchange rates, interest rates, and the price-control system. Steps were also taken to improve revenue, reduce domestic borrowing, and improve public-debt management.

A second structural adjustment programme in 1983–5 consisted of measures to improve the performance of productive sectors by reducing price controls and further boosting prices for smallholder crops. Improvements in the mobilization and management of resources and the strengthening of institutions were also called for. Consolidating and expanding gains made under earlier programmes was the focus of the third set of structural adjustment measures in 1985–7. The tasks set out included encouraging productivity, diversifying and promoting exports, and strengthening the government's ability to formulate and implement policies (World Bank, 1984).

Fiscal and monetary policy

To reduce the budget deficit, the programme contained a number of measures to increase revenue, mainly through upward adjustments in indirect taxes. Improved monitoring of expenditures was also called for. The deficit as percentage of GDP has been reduced but is still high.

To encourage savings and promote efficient allocation of resources, interest rates have been adjusted upward periodically. But these steps have been largely thwarted by high inflation rates that have kept real interest rates negative most of the time. Nominal rates could not be raised above current levels because that would discourage borrowing and adversely affect profitability of financial institutions and other enterprises, and strain the government budget by raising charges on the internal debt.

The country has had to rely on physical controls to check the level and allocation of bank credit: ceilings on the growth of credit, requests and moral suasion directed at the commercial banks. These have not always been successful. Transport disruption in 1979, for example, led to higher borrowing levels. And in the early 1980s commercial banks found it difficult to reduce credit to tobacco estates because they had to protect earlier investments.

Exchange rate and balance of payments

Since 1982 Malawi's currency has been devalued once or twice each year in order to stimulate exports, reduce demand for imports, and correct disequilibria in the balance of payments. Structural factors such as low elasticity of import demand have limited the impact of devaluation, however. Imports have declined because of physical controls and foreign-exchange shortages, not devaluation *per se*. High transport costs tend to reduce net export receipts. Other negative side effects of devaluation include high inflation and large increases in external private and public debt.

Expansion of non-traditional exports is hampered by the generally unfavourable world economic climate — protectionism, mounting competition from other developing countries, and sluggish growth. Import-substitution industrialization has likewise had a limited effect, owing to heavy reliance on importation of capital goods, intermediate goods, and raw materials. Its contribution to exports has been negligible. In future, import-substitution will be selective and will stress industries that minimize the use of imported inputs while maximizing the use of domestically produced ones.

Import liberalization

Phase one of import liberalization began in February 1988 and involved removal of exchange control procedures on a list of goods comprising about a quarter of the total import bill. These included fertilizer, petrol, and some 25 per cent of imported raw materials and spare parts.

Under the second phase, begun in August of the same year, the list was extended to cover 30 per cent of the import bill, including a further 50 per cent of imported raw materials and spares as well as a small number of intermediate goods. In effect, importers of these products need no longer obtain prior central bank approval for foreign allocation to listed goods. Further phases were planned and the programme was completed in 1990, at which time importation of most goods would have been liberalized. Most of the US$170 million donor support for the adjustment programmes will be used to finance these imports (*Africa Economic Digest*, 17–25 August 1988). Already imported materials for industry are more readily available and industry is reported operating at 50–60 per cent of capacity, up from 20–30 per cent before trade liberalization.

Price liberalization

Prices for a wide range of basic and luxury goods and services were decontrolled in 1983–5. Only petroleum, fertilizer, sugar, and meat remained subject to controls at that time, and since then meat prices, too, have been decontrolled. These changes have meant that firms can more readily make upward adjustments in prices in response to increased costs, enabling them to maintain profitability, save, and invest. But by giving businessmen a free hand, decontrol has also contributed significantly to high inflation rates, to the detriment of wage and salary earners and others whose incomes rise slowly.

Agriculture

All the stabilization and structural adjustment programmes have stressed the need to assure adequate incentives through price adjustments and the removal of subsidies on agricultural inputs. While the World Bank sought even larger relative increases in prices of export crops (tobacco, cotton, groundnuts) than for the staple food crop, maize, the authorities have repeatedly moved in the opposite direction (Kydd and

Hewitt, 1986). Thus the smallholder agricultural sector has remained basically a food producer, leaving export production to the estate sector. Limited availability of land and rising input costs have also constrained the transformation of smallholders into exporters.

The country produces enough food for its own needs in years of good rainfall. But this does not mean that all smallholding farmers produce enough food for their households. Those owning less than 0.7 hectares of land cannot be self-sufficient, and these make up 35 per cent of farm households. Among those who must acquire food by purchase and in other ways, there are also many who lack the means.

A phased removal of subsidies on fertilizer sold to smallholders was agreed to by the government and the World Bank. The removal began, but had to be slowed due to a large increase in the price of fertilizer that government did not want to pass on wholly to the farmers. To the extent that subsidies had already been reduced, smallholders were experiencing hardship, especially the poorer ones.

Institutional reforms

Restructuring has taken place at three parastate enterprises — Press Holdings, the Malawi Development Corporation (MDC), and Admarc. The latter is a trading corporation for agricultural produce. The financial position and performance of Press and the MDC have improved tremendously. With regard to Admarc, some of its bush markets have been closed down, the marketing of smallholder crops except for tobacco and cotton has been liberalized, and some of its commercial and industrial investments have been sold off.

The efficiency of Admarc has improved as a result, but the producers served by its bush markets were often those not served by private traders. Moreover, Admarc failed to buy enough maize during the first year of liberalized marketing to supply deficit areas. Private traders who offered higher prices bought more but lacked the infrastructure for storage and supply of needy areas. The prices they charged consumers were also exorbitant. In 1988 the system was changed to require private traders to sell maize to Admarc.

Impact of the Adjustment Measures

Introduction

Devaluation, price liberalization, debt-service obligations, and rising transport costs have all made public services more expensive. The public debt burden since 1979 has been especially heavy. In 1981–2, external debt service payments amounted to 25.8 per cent of recurrent government expenditures; the figure rose to 38.3 per cent in 1986–7. This has contributed to increases in the overall government budget deficit, the financing of which has entailed borrowing both at home – from the banking system – and abroad. Net of repayments, domestic borrowing was a greater source of funds than foreign borrowing in five of the nine fiscal years between 1979–80 and 1987–8. Most of this came from the central bank, with an expansionary impact on aggregate demand. Rising debt claims on the government budget have reduced the total resources available to public ministries and departments, and to that extent have limited people's access to social services.

Education

As a result of these budgetary constraints, spending on education as a percentage of total recurrent spending was lower in 1988–9 than in 1978–9. While spending per pupil more than doubled in nominal terms during the 1980s, inflation rendered this increase negligible. This is worrisome for several reasons. First, the involvement of non-governmental organizations in education in Malawi is minimal. Thus there is little substitution of private school education for public. Second, the expansion of enrolment at all levels that has occurred in the face of declining resource levels has meant that pupils and teachers have had fewer materials to work with and that pupil –teacher ratios have risen to unacceptably high levels. The average pupil–teacher ratio is 63 : 1, but more than 100 : 1 in certain areas. Many classrooms are grossly over-crowded. Third, overall coverage remains low despite the expansion of the educational system during the last quarter-century. The 1.15 million primary-school pupils amount to just 47 per cent of the 6–13 age group, and the 29,000 pupils in formal secondary schools amount to an enrolment level of just 4.5 per cent. Many children who begin school never achieve lasting literacy and numeracy. Drop-out and repetition rates are very high.

Health

Again, spending on health as a percentage of total recurrent spending was lower in 1988–9 than in 1978–9. While nominal spending per capita increased over the decade, real spending registered no gains and population growth outstripped such increases in service provision as there were.

Unlike in education, there is a significant amount of health-care involvement by non-governmental providers. Thus, while budgetary constraints have limited the delivery of services by the public sector, those provided by NGOs have partially filled the gap. Such replacement can only be partial, however, because of the limited presence of NGOs in certain areas of the country and because NGOs place charges on their services that many patients cannot afford.

Employment and unemployment

The employment data presented in Table 10.1 are incomplete in so far as they describe only formal-sector employment. At this writing, there are some 450,000 formal-sector jobs (185,000 in the estate sector), accounting for 14 per cent of the labour force. An additional 120,000 are estimated to be in the informal sector, and the remaining 2.9 million workers are smallholding farmers (World Bank, 1990). Data on formal-sector employment are fairly reliable as they are obtained through an official quarterly employment enquiry and from annual surveys of employment and earnings. The other data are based on estimates and as such are less reliable.

Unemployment data are more scanty. An estimated 130,000 persons are now looking for work, which implies an unemployment rate of 4 per cent. This figure is misleading to the extent that many persons who do not readily find urban employment return to the rural areas where they may be underemployed. Data on underemployment and other hidden forms of unemployment are not available.

Waged employment in the formal sector grew in Malawi at a rapid annual rate of 8.3 per cent between 1968 and 1977. This reflected a rapid rate of growth of output, facilitated in turn by a stable internal and external economic environment. Correspondingly, the rate of open unemployment in the country was low — 2 per cent overall in 1977, and 5 per cent in the urban sector, according to official census data.

Between 1977 and 1986, formal-sector employment grew at an average annual rate of only 3.7 per cent, reflecting the lower rate of expansion of output which was in turn the consequence of the unfavourable internal and external conditions discussed above.

Conclusions and Recommendations

Education

Public expenditure on education is projected to increase from about 12 per cent of total recurrent expenditure in 1989–90 to 15 per cent in 1993–4. Even if realized, this share will still be below that in many other African countries. There is a great need to increase the coverage of the education system, especially at the primary level. But maintaining and improving the quality of the existing system is still more important. More teaching materials and improved teaching methods are necessary. Larger increases in investment resources and recurrent spending will be required if the government's ambitious goals for the expansion of education are to be met by 1995 (World Bank, 1990).

Health

Public expenditure on health is projected to increase from 7 per cent of total recurrent expenditure in 1989–90 to about 9 per cent in 1993–4. Even if realized, this share will still be below that in many other African countries. As in education, there is a need to increase both investment and recurrent spending levels if the goal of health care for all is to be attained by the year 2000.

Top priority should be accorded to the control of malaria, the leading cause of admissions and death among hospital in-patients. A community-based system for presumptive treatment of malaria deserves serious consideration. Further investment in water supply, sanitation, and hygiene education should be undertaken to control diarrhea and other water-related diseases. Also deserving high priority are measures to prevent the spread of HIV infection (World Bank, 1990).

Improving child survival is critical to lowering overall mortality and increasing life expectancy. Child spacing is probably the most cost-effective approach to reducing infant mortality (World Bank, 1990). Equally if not more important are efforts to alleviate poverty and especially malnutrition, as are efforts to raise education levels, particularly among women. Mothers with primary education tend to have healthier and better-nourished children, lower fertility, and higher productivity (World Bank, 1990).

Employment

Rapid population growth combined with the economy's weakened capacity to absorb increasing numbers of workers presents a serious challenge. Between 1990 and 2015, the labour force is projected to grow from 3.5 million to nearly 8 million. The problem of creating more than 4 million new jobs during the next twenty-five years is a daunting one.

To absorb all new entrants into the labour force, formal-sector employment would have to grow at 20 per cent per year. This is not possible. Public-sector employment is likely to expand at only about 2 per cent per year. Private-sector employment growth will depend on the adoption of new labour-intensive, export-oriented, and import-substituting industries, and on the introduction of new crops and further processing of current estate crops. Considerable uncultivated land is available in the estate sector, and owners should also be encouraged to adopt improved technology and thereby create employment. Additional employment expansion will also depend on export prices and prospects, about which little is known at present.

Smallholder agriculture offers no scope for absorbing growing numbers of labour-force entrants. The main hindrance is growing pressure on arable land. Informal-sector employment growth is constrained by capital and credit availability, the small domestic market, licensing restrictions, limited access to foreign exchange, and inadequate entrepreneurial skills. Some programmes are already in place that address these problems. The compelling reasons for developing this sector are that the cost per job tends to be lower than in the more capital-intensive formal sector; import-dependence tends to be lower; and income elasticity of demand for the sector's output is high and positive (World Bank, 1990).

References

International Monetary Fund (1983). 'Malawi: Extended Fund Facility', *IMF Survey*. Washington, DC.
International Monetary Fund (1988a). 'Malawi: Enhanced Structural Adjustment Facility', *IMF Survey*. Washington, DC.
International Monetary Fund (1988b). 'Malawi Stand-by Arrangement', *IMF Survey*. Washington DC.
J. Kydd and A. Hewitt (1986). 'The Effectiveness of Structural Adjustment Lending: Initial Evidence from Malawi'. *World Development*, Vol. 14, No. 3: 347–65.
Malawi Government (1983). *International Conference of Partners in Economic Development: Past Performance and Prospects for 1983–7, Vol. 1*, p.16. Lilongwe: Department of Economic Planning and Development.
Malawi Government (1988). *Economic Report*. Lilongwe: Department of Economic Planning and Development.
Malawi Government (1989). *Economic Report*. Lilongwe: Department of Economic Planning and Development.
S. Nyirenda and C. M. Moyo (1990). *Malawi: Adjustment in the Education Sector*. Paper presented at workshop on the Effects of Structural Adjustment Programmes. Mangochi, 25 February – 2 March 1990.
World Bank (1981). *Malawi: Employment Aspects of Economic Development*. Washington, DC.
World Bank (1984). *Malawi: One of Africa's Success Stories*. Washington, DC.
World Bank (1989). *Sub-Saharan Africa: From Crisis to Sustainable Growth*. Washington, DC.
World Bank (1990). *Malawi Human Resource Development Study*. Washington, DC.

11 Cameroon

Wilfred A. Ndongko

The Economy after Independence

Following Cameroon's independence in 1960, economic development policies and programmes were oriented toward the expansion of the nation's industrial base, with the aim of providing substitutes for the products imported from the former colonial rulers (Ndongko, 1976). However, the country has remained largely tied to agriculture, particularly to the export of commodities widely produced elsewhere in Africa and still poorly regulated on the international market. The first five-year development plan (1960–5) failed to alter the existing distribution of resources between the different regions and sectors. The concentration of investment in the Littoral, already the most industrially developed region, only led to growing inter-regional disparities.

The 1966–71 plan aimed to eliminate gross disparities between the income of wage earners and peasants; termed the 'Peasant Plan', it established national agencies for land reform and rural development. Diversification of cash crops was projected to improve peasant export production. Besides the large quantities of cocoa, coffee, bananas, lumber, and cotton already being exported, it was hoped that production of tea, rubber, and palm products would be increased. The need for such diversification was especially acute in former West Cameroon, where a steady decline in banana production had been only partially offset by expansion in rubber, cocoa, palm oil, tea, and pepper (Cameroon, 1961). Under the second plan, Gross Domestic Product grew at an annual average rate of 4 per cent, twice that of the expansion under the first plan. Growth in the agricultural sector was particularly rapid, at an annual average rate of 11.1 per cent.

Cameroon registered modest but steady progress toward industrial development and diversification of the economy in the 1970s. The primary sector's relative contribution to GDP fell gradually, while those of the secondary and tertiary sectors rose. The proportion of GDP entering the market grew by some 2 per cent per year, indicating a relative decline in autonomous consumption among agricultural producers. The overall growth in GDP was shared out more or less as follows:

- administrative services became more demanding in comparison with other consumers;
- household consumption rose somewhat faster than did average overall consumption;
- the share of wages in total income (which stood at 31.5 per cent in 1960) increased by an average of 1.25 per cent a year; and
- incomes of agricultural producers stagnated.

As of 1980, about 34 per cent of Cameroon's GDP was derived from agriculture, fishing and forestry, and about 75 per cent of the population was still engaged in these sectors. Primary agricultural and forest products (plus minimally processed forms) constituted 57 per cent of 1980 exports (Cameroon, 1976). Cocoa and coffee alone accounted for 41 per cent of total exports; other significant products were timber, cotton, rubber, oil seeds, and bananas. In value terms, some 40 per cent of primary-sector output was exported; the remainder consisted primarily of foodstuffs consumed without further processing, along with a few inputs for manufacturing (e.g., palm oil, textiles, cigarettes, lumber).

While food production rose somewhat more rapidly than population through 1971, drought adversely affected production in 1972–4. Millet and sorghum were most seriously affected. Root crops and plantain output increased through 1976, but even so that year saw overall food production equal that of 1971 at best. Drought returned to some areas in 1977 and 1978. Bananas, beans, and starchy roots are staple products in the coastal and forest zones; groundnuts, millet, sorghum, lake fish, and livestock are typical of the savannah and Sahel regions; and maize and poultry are produced throughout the country. Food and beverage imports are dominated by rice, wheat, and amenity products for the upper-class market.

Industrial (non-artisan) and power production accounted for nearly 25 per cent of GDP by 1982, and domestic production was meeting about half the domestic demand for manufactured consumer goods. Much of the industrial share of GDP was taken up by aluminium smelting, based on imported alumina and amounting to the export of power. On the whole, Cameroon industry was not well integrated into the country's overall economic structure and provided only limited linkage or spread effects.

Until the 1980s, Cameroon remained relatively insulated from the convulsions of international economic crisis. Since 1982, however, the country has been hard hit. A particularly severe drought in 1982–3 coincided with a fall in energy production and corresponding difficulties for those industries that consume the largest amounts of power. The overall volume of exports declined, as did industrial output (the latter by 6 per cent). Raw material prices also began to deteriorate at this moment.

Even so, Cameroon's balance of trade remained in surplus in 1982–3. The economy turned upward through 1985 as favourable conditions reappeared and the country's principal trading partners experienced recovery. Prices of coffee and other cash crops also improved. The respite was short-lived, however: petroleum receipts dropped by 40 per cent in 1985–6, along with a general decrease of export revenues caused by declines in the value of the US dollar and in prices for coffee, cocoa, cotton, palm oil, and other cash crops. Meanwhile, expenditures on imports continued to rise due to inflated prices of manufactured goods. As a consequence the balance of trade surplus plunged, leading to an overall balance of payments deficit of 120 billion francs CFA in 1985–6. And as a further consequence of the international economic crisis, development assistance to Cameroon was drastically reduced.

The Structural Adjustment Programme

The onset of crisis

These shifts in the mid-1980s brought to light serious shortcomings in the domestic economic policies that had been pursued until then. The state, already engaged in a vast programme of investments, continued its expansionist approach on the demand side without taking the new trends into consideration. In 1986–7, despite continued production increases in most primary export products, the overall level of economic activity declined sharply. State revenue thus dropped by 16 per cent and the Special Development Fund was reduced to near zero, this at a time when expenditures and especially investments were still rising. The resulting deficit, estimated at 464,000 million CFA francs, was financed by the Central Bank through massive withdrawals from the country's deposit account and from those of public bodies with a sound position in the banking system. Also, arrears were allowed to accumulate in local transactions (BEAC, 1980). The current accounts deficit in the balance of payments was financed in part by short- and long-term borrowing but especially by accumulating a debit balance in the French Treasury operation account.

The growing financial demands of the state and state corporations led the banks to expand credit facilities (by more than 10 per cent in 1986–7) and to nearly double their foreign commitments. The latent solvency problems that had been developing as a consequence of the banks' chronically inadequate base of share capital, and their low profitability and weakened credibility with respect to foreign partners, suddenly became a severe liquidity crisis. Loans from foreign partners dropped by 26,000 million CFA francs between 1985–6 and 1986–7, and at the same time many individual depositors withdrew all or part of their funds. Foreign reserves in local banks fell from a surplus of 115,700 million CFA francs in December 1985 to a deficit of 8900 million CFA francs in August 1987 (Cameroon, 1988).

Inasmuch as current economic indicators showed no sign that a rapid economic recovery was in sight, it became absolutely necessary to re-establish macro-economic balance to the economy and to adjust production costs and structures in order to enhance performance and competitiveness in an improved institutional environment. The 1987–8 Finance Law was the first step: it reduced projected budget revenue by 19 per cent; placed ceilings on personnel expenditures; mandated systematic retirement of personnel exceeding age limits set by the Public Service Corporations; increased taxes on petroleum products, beer, alcohol, other beverages, cigarettes, and certain imported luxury goods; and set up a special State Revenue Collection Commission (Cameroon, 1988).

In the light of the magnitude of economic imbalance and the extensive resources required to restore equilibrium and boost recovery, the government decided to seek assistance from the World Bank, the International Monetary Fund, and friendly governments. A Structural Adjustment Programme was drawn up by the Cameroon government and negotiated with the World Bank and IMF. The programme reflects the country's firm resolve to implement coherent global and sectoral strategies aimed at satisfying, first of all, the basic needs of Cameroonians.

Objectives and measures of structural adjustment

Implementation began with the 1988–9 fiscal year. The main objectives combine the progressive reduction of constraints impeding economic activity with a reorientation of the role of the state and of public services toward programmes to improve both the welfare and productivity of all citizens. In this way it is hoped that the social impact of the adjustment programme will be taken into account. Along with reducing the annual inflation rate to 3 per cent and fostering GDP growth of 3 per cent per annum, there are four principal aims (BERD, 1988):

- stabilization and restructuring of public finance, with the deficit to decline progressively and disappear by the end of 1991–2;
- reduction of the current accounts deficit in the balance of payments from 125,000 million CFA francs in 1988–9 to 100,000 million CFA francs in 1991–2;
- restructuring of public corporations; and
- restructuring and stabilization of the monetary and financial system.

Fiscal policy aims at reducing public expenditures and demand for imported goods while increasing budget revenue. Expenditure reductions will focus on freezing salaries, limiting the impact of advancements in rank, and otherwise restructuring salaries and benefits to state personnel; reducing embassy staffs and limiting the recruitment of new personnel elsewhere in the public sector; and reducing subsidies to state corporations. In terms of increasing revenue, charges and duties collected for various public services and licences are to be revised; value-added (VAT) and real-estate taxes are to be introduced; and the income tax system and fiscal services generally are to be improved. Considering the fact that Cameroon belongs to the Franc Zone and that it finds itself in a quite precarious financial situation, the following monetary measures are envisioned: restructuring the banking sector, including the possible liquidation and rehabilitation of certain banks; reduction of the number of different rates; increase of the authorized banking margin; steps toward the abolition of interest-rate subsidies; and progressive replacement of direct monetary control measures with indirect ones.

To insure that the external debt remains within limits compatible with the economy's capacity to generate enough revenue to repay loans, the government seeks to limit the annual increase of the debt to 3.5 per cent of GDP; this will enable the state to contain debt service to about 25 per cent of budget revenue.

On the supply side, price liberalization will be implemented to provide incentives to the economy. Agricultural producers will be remunerated on the basis of prices to suppliers, along with a bonus calculated according to world-market prices. Trade liberalization will involve legal revisions to facilitate commercial activity, a gradual loosening of restrictions on imports, and the simplification of import procedures.

Public investment policy is to be reoriented along the following lines: granting priority to projects primarily aimed at stimulating production, especially those involving joint financing; completing priority activities already under way; and abandoning the procedure of bringing forward credits not fully utilized during previous activities and projects.

Within the framework of this strategy, the private sector is expected to intervene more vigorously in investment and production, thereby progressively replacing the public sector in several areas that up to now have been reserved to the state. The Investment Code will be revised with this aim in view.

In the face of fluctuating raw material prices, Cameroon will direct efforts toward developing export sectors that constitute a viable alternative capable of gaining new markets. The industrial sector will be restructured so as to improve the quantitative performance of the economy, intensify inter-industrial relations, and minimize the balance of trade deficit. In the agricultural sector, research and dissemination services will be reinforced, cooperatives will be encouraged to play their deserved role, and the management of agro-industrial concerns will be reformed.

Initial consequences

It should be pointed out that the implementation of the structural adjustment measures, particularly in the banking sector (where four out of the ten banks have been closed) and the cash-crop sector (notably the National Produce Marketing Board), has resulted in considerable retrenchment. For example, the restructuring of the banks and the marketing board resulted in the dismissal of some 200 employees at Paribas-Cameroon, more than 400 at the Cameroon Bank, 300 at the Cameroon Development Bank, more than 400 at the National Fund for Rural Development, 900 at the National Produce Marketing Board, and some 1000 (out of a total of 1500) at the Société Camerounaise de Banque (IMF, 1989). The banks that closed down (Cameroon Bank, Société Camerounaise de Banque, Cameroon Development Bank and the Paribas Bank) accounted for an estimated 36 per cent of the banking system's balance sheet and 41 per cent of its non-performing assets. One of these banks, the Société Camerounaise, was reopened after restructuring its balance sheet. It is now under the majority control of the Credit Lyonnaise, previously a minority foreign partner.

In the cash-crop sector (coffee, cotton, cocoa), adjustment measures have involved reductions in producer prices, the settlement of arrears, and a redefinition of the role of the marketing boards. For cocoa, producer prices were cut by an average of 40 per cent. These cuts, made necessary by the fall in world market prices, have been mitigated to an extent by the suspension of export taxes for cocoa and coffee, by a 20 to 25 per cent reduction in traders' margins, and by reforms designed to reduce operating costs in marketing and extension services.

Social Consequences of Structural Adjustment

In view of the real and potential negative socio-economic consequences of structural adjustment, the Cameroon government, in collaboration with the World Bank, has set forth a Social Dimensions of Adjustment Project (SDA) that calls for a series of measures in the health, education, and employment sectors with a view to mitigating these adverse effects. A February 1990 meeting in Paris between Cameroon authorities, international finance institutions and donor countries resulted in commitments of some US$85 million for financing SDA, distributed as follows: World Bank, 6 million CFA francs; African Development Bank, 4.5 million CFA francs; Federal Republic of Germany, 2000 million CFA francs; United States, 2000 million CFA francs; and Canada, 1000 million CFA francs. A further World Bank loan of US$20 million will also contribute to financing the SDA (*Jeune Afrique Economie*, 1990).

The overall goals of the SDA include:

- re-establishing a positive per capita growth rate in the medium term;
- improving the indicators of living conditions (e.g., number of inhabitants per hospital bed and per doctor, number of pupils per teacher and per classroom, life expectancy); and
- developing Cameroonians' capacity to improve their own living standards through personal effort.

Health and health care

In its statement on Development Strategy and Economic Recovery that accompanied the Structural Adjustment Programme, the Cameroon government has set priority on the promotion of preventive and primary health care, especially in rural areas; improvement in training of health-care personnel; and rationalization of the referral system. Specific steps are to include re-equipping and revitalizing basic facilities, and strengthening curative and preventive services in the priority areas of immunization, primary health care, communicable tropical diseases, and sexually transmitted diseases (STD) including AIDS. The institutional capacity of the Ministry of Health (MINSANTÉ) for strategic planning, programming and budgeting, financial management and coordination of sector operations is to be strengthened.

The action programme to implement this perspective involves a series of measures. To ensure the availability of essential generic drugs and to reduce the unit costs of basic health services, the government will institute a cost-recovery programme and take charge of purchasing and distributing medical and pharmaceutical supplies, stocks of which have run down since 1986 owing to budget constraints. Such supplies will support programmes of primary health care, health education, immunization, and prevention and treatment of STDs. Health centres and first-level referral hospitals are to be re-equipped.

To ensure that the population, especially in rural areas, takes advantage of the upgraded primary health-care services, an integrated education and communication programme will foster greater awareness of available services and their uses, promote early recourse to health care, and encourage preventive personal and community health practices. With regard to STDs and AIDS in particular, the action programme aims at sensitizing the population about the prevention of such diseases, reducing AIDS transmission through blood transfusion, monitoring the evolution of the epidemic in high risk groups, and improving technical knowledge.

Educational campaigns and training workshops will be undertaken, supplies for rapid HIV tests will be provided, and various forms of institutional care for AIDS patients will be evaluated.

The action programme will also support efforts to improve immunization coverage among children and women of childbearing age. This will involve personnel training and the equipping of health facilities with refrigerators, vaccines, and vehicles so as to facilitate regular vaccinations. The goal is 85 per cent immunization coverage for children under 20 months of age by 1994, by which date 1000 fully operational and sustainable immunization centres are to be in place nationwide.

The overall cost of this health module within the SDA project will amount to US$12.66 million, distributed as follows: policy design, $320,000; primary health care, $4.61 million; information, $500,000; STD/AIDS, $350,000; immunization, $3.08 million; operations and maintenance, $1.11 million; institutional strengthening, $1.77 million; and module management, $920,000.

Education

The government's stated goals in the education sector are to maintain the quantitative achievements in primary education, improve educational quality at all levels, and improve the system's relevance to the country's economic and social development needs. To these ends the government is undertaking an action programme designed to strengthen the institutional capacities of the education ministries and replenish supplies depleted as a result of budget cuts in prior years.

The education sector is managed at the primary level by the Ministère de l'Education Nationale (MINEDUC) and at the secondary and university levels by the Ministère de l'Enseignement Supérieur et de la Recherche Scientifique (MESIRES). A task force drawn from both ministries as well as from the University of Yaoundé and other ministries involved with training activities has been established to prepare and implement a medium-term strategy containing specific reform measures. Among the key areas to be addressed are:

- improvement in the efficiency of the allocation of resources to the sector and, within the sector, of the resources allocated to primary education as compared to other levels;
- improvement in the management of financial and human resources;
- strengthening the linkages between education, training, and the employer community, with a view to increasing the relevance of programmes to the country's socio-economic needs;
- improvements in student performance and, in this context, the merits of combining various aspects of the dual-language (French and English) education system and the implications for the quality of the teacher force; and
- improvements in access to education by women and by minority groups.

While medium- to long-term reforms of the education system are being prepared, priority programmes must be protected. To this end, the SDA project will finance an immediate injection of badly needed materials and other pedagogical inputs for primary and secondary schools. To begin to meet a very large backlog of pressing needs, the government has allocated 3 billion CFA francs (US$9.4 million), of which 47 per cent is to go to primary education, 32 per cent to technical secondary education, and 21 per cent to general secondary education. This one-time allocation will partially compensate for non-personnel cuts in the education budget since 1986 and is consistent with the government's stated priority of promoting universal basic education among children 6 to 14 years of age as well as strengthening the teaching of science and technical subjects.

Priority in allocation of funds would be accorded to: (1) primary schools, (2) schools in rural areas and in disadvantaged neighbourhoods of Yaoundé and Douala, and (3) schools with a predominantly female student population. Some 500 schools are to receive desks, textbooks, and other materials. Twenty technical schools will receive materials for workshops and equipment for libraries. And some 225 general secondary schools will receive materials for their science laboratories.

Adoption of a new educational policy will also require institutions in this sector to improve their management capacity. As part of the Education and Professional Training Project, the government will strengthen the planning divisions of MINEDUC and MESIRES and create a small planning unit at the University of Yaoundé. A new programme budgeting system and a budget monitoring process will respond to the priorities defined in the new policy.

The overall cost of this education module within the SDA project will amount to US$8.55 million, with $7.5 million devoted to investment and $1.0 million to meet recurrent expenditures.

Employment

Unemployment is a central preoccupation of the Cameroon authorities. Even during the years of strong economic growth (1977–86), there were probably more people who reached working age than were absorbed by the labour market. After the onset of the economic crisis, the situation worsened considerably as income declined and the modern private sector contracted. Under structural adjustment the situation becomes still more acute as public enterprises and banks are shut down or cut back, public services are not allowed to expand, and thus the principal sources of jobs for new graduates of secondary schools and the university cease to exist. It is estimated that well over 30,000 persons are being added to the ranks of the unemployed as a result of structural adjustment.

The employment component of the SDA project seeks to address these problems through measures aimed at improving the functioning of the labour market and promoting the creation of new employment. The socio-economic groups targeted by these measures are employees of the private, public, and parapublic sectors who will be unemployed during the transitional phase of structural adjustment; young graduates and drop-outs from the educational system; and the most impoverished and vulnerable sectors of the population, including unskilled women and young persons with insufficient resources to undertake self-employment.

Toward these ends, the National Employment Fund (FNE) has been created as a largely autonomous administrative body with a twelve-member board, five of whose members represent the private sector and five the interested ministries. The FNE will finance five principal activities:

- systematic collection of information on training and job opportunities, and distribution of that information;

- strengthening of formal vocational training;
- support for on-the-job training;
- support for individual initiatives aimed at self-employment; and
- advisory and financial support for the creation and expansion of micro-enterprises.

The Project will also finance studies that will contribute to the future development of national policy in the employment sector and help to reinforce the planning capacity of the labour ministry. A National Manpower Survey, initiated earlier by the Ministry of Labour and Social Security but suspended for lack of funds, will be completed.

The National Employment Fund will be 85 per cent financed by external donors, and the government will provide the remaining 15 per cent. The total investment and recurrent costs of US$31.06 million is to be allocated as follows:

Employment and training assistance	0.80
Formal training	5.90
On-the-job training	4.39
Self-employment	10.08
Micro-enterprises	6.38
Administrative costs	3.51

The FNE's Employment and Training Assistance Division will collect data on training and employment opportunities and offer advisory services to job seekers. Its main clients are expected to be persons laid off from public-sector enterprises closed or reorganized under the structural adjustment programme and secondary-school and university graduates unable to find jobs directly. It is expected that between 5000 and 6000 job seekers a year will be serviced. The main office will be in Yaoundé, where a majority of those discharged by public enterprises are to be found, but additional units will be located in Douala and other cities as needed.

Many job seekers will already have basic skills, but a significant number will need to be directed to formal vocational training centres. The FNE will support such centres either by providing resources to co-finance the fees required of individual trainees, or else by direct financing of the expansion of selected centres. The FNE's on-the-job training programme will finance part of the cost of training new recruits into enterprises in both the modern and informal sectors. Candidates for the modern sector will normally be former state enterprise employees who are already professionally experienced and need only retraining in new skills or technologies to qualify for jobs in private enterprises. Candidates for the informal sector will be mainly young, first-time job seekers with few resources and little access to the labour market. FNE contributions to training costs will be higher for firms that agree beforehand to hire the trainees at the end of the training period.

The self-employment programme targets young graduates from vocational and technical schools and from higher education, as well as laid-off employees. It will provide small grants of up to 1.5 million CFA francs (US$5000) to generate at least one job (in the first instance, the job seeker's own), subject to presentation of a credible business plan. Employees receiving separation payments from previous employers will be expected to contribute those to the capitalization of the new business.

The micro-enterprise support programme will target job seekers with entrepreneurial skills and at least a modicum of financial resources whose projects are deemed capable of generating up to five jobs. The programme will also extend financial support on a grants basis to non-governmental organizations and other groups that can provide training or advisory services to start or expand micro-enterprises. The FNE will not itself take on credit activities but will assure refinancing of credits to micro-enterprises of up to 20 million CFA francs (US$65,000) made on market terms by financial institutions. Cameroon has made several unsuccessful attempts to support the development of small businesses, so the FNE will enter this field very cautiously and on a small scale, with an initial two-year pilot project. Nonetheless, creation and expansion of such small businesses is critical to the Cameroonian economy.

Conclusions and Recommendations

Within the framework of the franc zone, Cameroon is linked to France not through the Banque de France but through an Operations Account with the French Treasury. Hence the monetary and financial problems Cameroon currently faces may not be solved with the advent of Europe 1992. This is because other members of the European Community will continue to regard Cameroon's relations with France as bilateral and not the subject of negotiations within the framework of ACP–EC relations. Cameroon will again find itself unable to implement the monetary and financial policies necessary for structural adjustment and economic recovery, particularly with regard to the social dimension.

Moreover, the economic crisis manifests itself in Cameroon in subtle forms. Unless the country is able to redirect a substantial share of its resources into improvements in agricultural productivity in the traditional sector, to organize improved health services, to boost literacy, and to upgrade other such social amenities, little progress will be made during the implementation of structural adjustment. Needless to say, a high degree of political commitment and rigorous economic management will be required.

Economic growth under the terms of the structural adjustment programme and the Sixth Five-Year Development Plan will depend largely on whether or not within the urban, commercial, industrial, banking and insurance sectors the measures taken not only reduce the effect of the crisis but also improve existing socio-economic conditions and encourage the overall structural transformation of the economy.

Cameroon's structural adjustment programme was launched only in 1988–9; hence it would be premature to make any definitive evaluation of its success or failure. These will be determined largely by internal and external political and economic factors. Nonetheless, it can be said that if there is sufficient political will on the part of the Cameroon authorities, and total and unreserved support from external bilateral and multilateral organizations and foreign governments, the projected adjustment programme should be able to get Cameroon out of its present economic crisis.

References

BEAC (1980). *Rapport des Comités monétaires de la Banque des Etats d'Afrique Centrale.* Yaoundé: BEAC.

BERD & BAD (1988). *Plan de stabilization : aide mémoire sur la politique économique financière du Gouvernement camerounais, Juin 1988.* BERD, BAD.

Cameroon (1961). *Premier Plan quinquennal de développement économique et social.* Yaoundé: Ministère des Finances et du Plan.

Cameroon (1970, 1976). *Third and Fourth Five-Year Development Plans, 1970/1–1975/6 and 1976/7–1980/1.* Yaoundé: Ministry of Economic Affairs and Planning.

Cameroon (1988). *Rapport de synthèse de discussions Banque mondiale–Banque africaine de développement.*

IMF (1989). *Cameroon: Second Review under Stand-by Arrangement.* Washington, DC.

Jeune Afrique Economie (1990). No. 130 (April): 59.

W. A. Ndongko (1976). 'An Appraisal of the Cameroon Development Policy: 1960–70'. In *RTIEEF,* Yaoundé: Ministry of Finance.

12 Zaire

M. Lututala, M. Kintambu
& M. Mvudi

Introduction

In 1983, Zaire embarked on a vigorous structural adjustment programme preceded by three confirmation agreements. Another programme was concluded in 1987 for a three-year period but it was not pursued because of Zaire's non-observance of the commitments enshrined in the programme. These agreements and programmes were aimed at correcting the macro-economic imbalances which emerged after 1975 owing both to the decline in the price of copper on the world market and the results of the measures of 'Zaireanization' (nationalization) and radicalization (state control) of the marketing and production structures. However, Zaire did not honour its commitments under these programmes because of their negative impact on the social sectors. To our knowledge, no study has yet demonstrated this negative impact. Our aim is to attempt such an exercise, with the hope that it will give rise to more thorough studies in the future, once better statistics, which are now virtually non-existent, become available. After describing the major outlines of the trends in the Zairean economy from 1970 to 1990, we present the principal structural adjustment measures which were taken and strive to demonstrate the negative impact of these measures on health, education and employment. We conclude with some suggestions and recommendations.

The Zairean Economy, 1970–90

Between 1970 and 1990 the Zairean economy was marked by four major periods:

1   A period of expansion from 1970 to 1974, which actually started in 1968. This period was characterized by a high growth rate in which the marketed GDP increased on average by more than 4 per cent per annum. However, with the implementation of the Zaireanization measures adopted in the last quarter of 1973, the expansion suddenly ended in 1974, with a real growth rate of 0.34 per cent, as against 7.58 per cent the preceding year.

* Translated from the French original.

130

2   A crisis period from 1975 to 1982. The marketed GDP declined by about 6 per cent in 1975 and 1976 respectively, and fell on average by 4.31 per cent a year between 1974 and 1978. The overall budget deficit, inflation, and arrears on external debt reached an unprecedented level following the sharp drop in copper price in 1974. The decline in production was particularly sharp in the agro-industrial field – the principal victim of the Zaireanization and radicalization policies (Department of Agriculture and Rural Development, 1987: 1–8). A slight economic recovery was observed from 1979, when the marketed GDP increased by 0.15 per cent. This continued until 1981. But the following year the situation again deteriorated, with a sudden 3.84 per cent decline in GDP, compared to an increase of 2.84 per cent in 1981.

3   A period of stabilization and adjustment programmes concluded with the IMF and World Bank, lasting from 1983 through 1987. The deterioration of the economy had led Zaire to seek assistance from the two Bretton Woods institutions, resulting in the negotiation of a vigorous stabilization programme covering the period 1983–6, a key element of which was reform of the exchange system. Over this three-year period, the average marketed GDP growth rate rose to 2.68 per cent per year. In 1987 Zaire concluded a three-year structural adjustment programme with the IMF and World Bank, aimed at attaining an annual growth rate of around 3 per cent. Due to Zaire's non-observance of the programme's obligations, that objective was not attained, and the 1987 rate stood at only 2.32 per cent.

4   The post-programme crisis period, which started in 1988. Zaire's failure to meet its commitments led the IMF and World Bank to suspend their financial interventions, and also brought a break in relations with other major financial partners, such as Belgium and the United States. Zaire updated its economic programme in 1988 and 1989, but this failed to resolve the situation. In 1989 the marketed GDP growth rate went negative, at –0.48 per cent, and the economic situation has continued to deteriorate with each passing year.

Public finance

Zaire derives its revenues from three major sources: the Gecamines, tax and customs revenues collected by the Direction générale des contributions (the General Tax Revenues Office), and OFIDA. The mining industry's contribution to public revenues, which stood at 41.4 per cent in the early 1970s, declined sharply to 19.3 per cent in 1983–6, while tax revenues increased from 28 per cent in 1970–4 to 45.3 per cent in 1983–6. This improvement in the mobilization of tax revenues was due to the rigorous enforcement of the measures taken within the stabilization programmes supported by the IMF and the World Bank. But the collection of taxes relaxed after 1986, so that its contribution to budget revenues fell to 35.7 per cent in 1987–9, causing a shortfall in the Public Treasury.

Zaire's public expenditure is mainly charged to current expenditure, comprising staff remunerations, the operation of services, and debt servicing; the latter burden is considerable because of past investments in unproductive projects. The share of current expenditure in total public expenditure stood at 70 per cent in 1970–4, increasing to 77 per cent in 1975–82, 92 per cent in 1983–6, and 82 per cent in 1987–9. Some have deplored what they see as a lack of discipline in the management of budgetary expenditures, and especially in the favour shown to expenditures dictated by political and administrative purposes, as well as to investments with little or no economic return.

Inflation

In 1970–4, the average inflation rate was 11.3 per cent, rising to 59.1 per cent in 1975–9, then falling slightly to 47.2 per cent in 1980–2 and 46.5 per cent in 1983–6. Domestic prices then shot up to an average of 118.4 per cent between 1987 and 1990, after Zaire abandoned the structural adjustment programme. The rise in domestic prices in Zaire has been caused by several internal and external factors, among them: chronic overspending beyond budgetary forecasts, with deficit generally financed through the issue of new bank notes; the steady deterioration of the Zaire (the Zairean currency), against foreign currencies; a supply and demand imbalance of goods on the markets, but especially between foreign currencies; and the cost of oil products. The most direct consequence of inflation has been the fall in the purchasing power of workers and of the population as a whole, since the price increases precede and are much higher than salary increases. It can be reckoned that over the entire period under study, 1970 to 1990, prices increased at an average annual rate of 56.4 per cent, as against 48.4 per cent and 36.1 per cent for nominal salaries in private and public sectors, respectively. As a result, real salaries declined. In the public sector they fell by an average of 14.2 per cent per year between 1971 and 1990, except for a slight increase in real civil service salaries during the period of the IMF and World Bank programme. Similarly, private sector salaries fell by an average 5.8 per cent a year in real terms over the same two decades, interrupted by a temporary pause between 1979 and 1986, when they increased 14.9 per cent, on average.

Economic and Financial Adjustment Programmes

Following the rapid deterioration of the economic situation during 1974–6, the government was compelled to negotiate a confirmation agreement with the IMF. This lasted for one year, from May 1976 to May 1977, and was aimed at correcting balance of payments disequilibria, reducing external payments arrears, and stabilizing domestic prices. The programme did not attain its objectives. The aggregate deficit in the balance of payments was not re-absorbed in line with forecasts, because of a dwindling of export revenues from mining, caused by transportation and supply difficulties. With the weakening of the exchange position, outstanding arrears increased and imports remained insufficient. Furthermore, an excessive monetary financing policy spurred inflation to 80 per cent.

Faced with these disquieting results, another confirmation agreement followed. Set to cover the April 1977 to April 1978 period, it also sought to contain the balance-of-payments deficit and reduce inflation, while reviving economic activity and ensuring sufficient imported goods. But it too recorded very limited results. The balance of payments deficit fell only slightly, while the payments difficulties, coupled with the absence of a debt rescheduling agreement, drove up debt arrears. The authorities responded by printing more money, at twice the rate of the year before. The agreement was suspended, with only 5 million SDRs actually drawn, out of the total 45 million SDRs originally available.

Notwithstanding these difficulties, the authorities drew up a three-year development plan called the 'Mobutu Plan'. Its objectives were to reorganize the transport system, develop agriculture, optimize mining, decentralize economic activity by regions, and improve management. Within its framework a new investments code was published in September 1979, extending the scope of tax advantages to investors; a Minimum Agricultural Programme (PAM) was prepared in May 1984, aimed at boosting agricultural output in the short term; and there was a liberalization of the marketing of precious materials, especially gold and traditionally produced diamonds, which had generally been smuggled out of the country.

Concurrently, a third confirmation agreement was negotiated for 118 million SDRs, to cover the period August 1979 to February 1981. With its more rigorous application, some signs of improvement emerged in 1980, namely: a reduction in the balance of payments deficit; a reduction in the inflation rate, from 149.4 per cent in 1979 to 56.7 per cent in 1980; and an appreciable increase in GDP to 2.33 per cent in 1980, as against 0.25 per cent the preceding year. In spite of these encouraging trends, it was observed that attention was being focused increasingly on mining production, to the detriment of agricultural output. Thus the country became even more dependent on the production and export of minerals, particularly copper. An extended mechanism was then agreed with the IMF, to cover the June 1982 to June 1983 period. Although it was for 912 million SDRs, only 175 million were actually drawn, as the agreement was soon cancelled due to non-observance of the performance criteria.

The period 1983–6 was characterized by rigorous economic and monetary policies, negotiated within the framework of structural adjustment programmes signed with the IMF. These programmes aimed at a free and open convertibility of currency, a progressive liberalization of the economy, compliance with debt payment discipline, greater budgetary discipline, and continued efforts at rehabilitating public enterprises. In an effort to secure the success of these programmes, Zaire was able to negotiate with the Paris Club of official creditors a rescheduling of external debt payments estimated at 747 million SDRs. Moreover, an interim Economic Rehabilitation Programme was designed, providing for greater public investments. Thanks to rigorous policies, price liberalization and exchange rate measures, and trade in gold and diamonds, a net recovery in productive and commercial activity was observed up to December 1985. Decline then set in once more, due mainly to the poor management of public enterprises, poor planning, and an unfavourable economic environment.

Surveying the rather meagre results of these stabilization and public investment programmes, the government decided that henceforth, any programme with the IMF would be designed as a supplement to national efforts and be aimed at a genuine economic revival, not merely at austerity and stabilization. It also decided that Zaire's development be pursued through a five-year development plan, elaborated for the period 1986–90. This five-year plan was too ambitious, however, and projected obtaining 55.5 per cent of its financing from external sources. Despite some modifications, it was therefore not really carried out. Consequently, another structural adjustment programme was concluded for the period May 1987 to April 1990. As we noted earlier, Zaire's non-observance of its commitments led the IMF and World Bank to suspend their intervention in 1988.

In general, it can be said that the series of stabilization and structural adjustment programmes have registered only a limited success. The reasons are mainly:

1 the narrow concern for meeting their rigorous conditions only in order to obtain external aid and gain some debt relief;
2 the search for 'cyclical' solutions, while in fact the economic problems of Zaire are largely structural;
3 the lack of enthusiasm aroused by these programmes among the population.

The remainder of this study analyses the social impact of the structural adjustment programmes, in the context of Zaire's extraverted and underdeveloped economy.

Impact of Structural Adjustment Measures in Zaire

Evaluating the impact of structural adjustment programmes (SAPs) can be a delicate and a hazardous exercise. It has been conceded that structural adjustment measures can have negative repercussions on vulnerable population groups, at least in the short term (World Bank, 1989: 115). But demonstrating this can be problematic. At a conceptual level, the question arises as to how to distinguish between the impact of earlier unfavourable economic policies on a given social sector and the impact of a SAP measure designed to correct those policies. At an empirical level, the data may simply be too uncertain or partial. Reliable data are rare not only in Zaire, but also in other African countries. It is for this reason that the World Bank, out of its concern to reduce the social costs of structural adjustment, has over the past few years been conducting standard of living surveys.

Pending the availability of better data for Zaire, we shall employ secondary data derived from hospital registers, World Bank reports, and some studies on the areas of interest to us. Among other deficiencies, it should be kept in mind that these data do not relate to the entire Zairean population.

Current expenditures

In recent years, including the period of structural adjustment, the educational, health and agricultural sectors have benefited from a considerable increase in capital expenditures. However, this mainly reflected an increase in investment expenditure, and while beneficial in the long term, nevertheless came at the cost of immense sacrifices, including a reduction in current or operating expenditures. This latter point is illustrated in Table 12.1.

In contrast to capital expenditure, current expenditures in health, education and agriculture were very low during the structural adjustment period. In fact, for education, it was the lowest level recorded over the entire period, with its share in the government's current expenditure plummeting from 22.7 per cent in 1975–82 to 0.7 per cent in 1983–6, during structural adjustment, then subsequently rising to 2.2 per cent from 1987 to 1989. In health, the share of current expenditure devoted to this

Table 12.1. Shares of some social sectors in current expenditure (%)

Sector	1970–4	1975–82	1983–6	1987–9
Health	3.5	4.0	1.2	0.6
Education	25.3	22.7	0.7	2.2
Agriculture	1.7	2.1	0.4	0.2
Public debt	13.8	14.6	47.7	27.1

Source: Bank of Zaire, Annual Reports.

sector continued to decline, going from 4 per cent in 1975–82 to 0.6 per cent in 1987–9, with the sharpest portion of the drop coming during the adjustment period. A similar trend was observed in agriculture. This fall in current expenditure in the social sectors seems connected with the efforts to repay the public debt, which received the highest allocations precisely during the years of the programmes supported by the IMF and the World Bank.

The health sector

To show the impact of structural adjustment on health in Zaire, we shall consider, in the light of available data, two variables: the prevalence of diseases and the quality of medical care. Concerning the prevalence of diseases, we shall focus on two categories: infectious and parasitic diseases (tuberculosis, malaria, diarrhoea, various infections, gastro-enteritis, AIDS) on the one hand, and nutritional and metabolic diseases on the other. Most of these diseases (with the exception of AIDS) can be prevented by vaccination, public and domestic hygiene, and good food. Their prevalence can therefore be attributed to precarious or deteriorating living conditions, and inadequate health and sanitation services.

The following table provides some information on the causes of death among adults (20–59 years) in three hospitals in Kinshasa between 1981 and 1987. These are the General Hospital (Mama Yemo, 2000 beds), the Kintambo Hospital (454 beds), and the University Clinics (630 beds).

It can be observed that infectious and parasitic diseases have become even more frequent and deadly in the three hospitals. Since they cause death and do not merely give rise to cases of illness, the increasing fatalities associated with these diseases demonstrate the inability of health institutions to cure them. The impact that structural adjustment may have had can be identified by examining the situation before and after such programmes were adopted. In 1981, before SAP, the proportion of those suffering from infectious and parasitic diseases and who subsequently died was clearly lower in all three hospitals than after structural adjustment was initiated. At the General Hospital (Mama Yemo), for example, the percentages rose from 24 per cent in 1981 to 50 per cent in 1984 and 69 per cent in 1987. In the two other hospitals the increase was slightly less between 1981 and 1984, but more significant between 1984 and 1987.

Concerning nutritional and metabolic diseases, the general trend was also sharply upward between 1981 and 1987. But these diseases seem less prevalent. This may be because the table concerns only adults (20–59 years), who are relatively less prone to

Table 12.2 Causes of death, by percentage, among adults in three Kinshasa hospitals, 1981, 1984 and 1987

	1981			1984			1987		
	(1)	(2)	(3)	(1)	(2)	(3)	(1)	(2)	(3)
1. Infectious and parasitic diseases	15	50	24	18	59	50	33	71	69
2. Tumours	5	–	1	9	1	1	6	–	–
3. Endocrinal (hormone), nutritional and metabolic diseases	1	–	2	1	2	1	2	4	11
4. Blood diseases	2	3	13	4	1	5	1	–	–
5. Mental disorders	7	–	2	10	–	1	7	–	–
6. Diseases related to the nervous system and organs of feeling	6	2	12	6	2	10	4	5	10
7. Diseases of circulatory system	9	5	5	9	5	4	6	7	–
8. Diseases of respiratory tract	2	10	20	4	3	16	2	3	6
9. Diseases of the digestive system	1	12	3	6	7	2	7	6	1
10. Genito-urinary diseases	5	3	1	9	1	0	2	–	–
11. Skin diseases	–	–	–	–	–	–	1	–	–
12. Diseases of the osteo-muscular system	–	–	–	–	1	1	–	3	–
13. Poorly defined symptoms and disease conditions	38	13	12	19	4	8	26	–	–
14. Accidents, poisoning and traumatisms	9	2	5	6	14	1	3	1	3
TOTAL	100	100	100	100	100	100	100	100	100

(1) University Clinics
(2) Kintambo Hospital
(3) General Hospital
Source: Files of patients, compiled by E. Bobwa (1988).

such maladies. To better reflect the impact on nutritional and metabolic diseases, we should rather examine infant mortality, for which we have data on certain diseases at the Kalembelembe Pediatric Hospital in Kinshasa (Table 12.3). It emerges from this table that, from 1982 to 1986, malnutrition was the greatest cause of death among children. Not only did it remain the most deadly of all the illnesses, but it also took an increasingly severe toll, with mortality from malnutrition climbing from 16 per cent in 1982 to 44 per cent in 1986. More particularly, it was during the SAP period that the rates reflected the greatest upsurge, going from a 'stable' level of 9.6 per cent in 1983 to an all-time high of 44.4 per cent in 1986.

Table 12.3 Mortality rates of certain diseases at the Kalembelembe Pediatric Hospital, Kinshasa

Principal diagnosis	1982	1983	1984	1985	1986
Malnutrition	16.1	9.6	20.0	42.5	44.4
Measles	13.0	14.0	15.0	32.0	18.0
Diarrhoea	16.1	21.4	10.0	34.5	23.7
Respiratory diseases	9.7	12.6	7.9	28.9	21.2
Malaria	10.3	12.0	20.7	31.0	11.1
Anaemia	8.3	0.0	0.0	33.3	10.0
Meningitis	8.5	8.1	6.6	21.1	14.1
Digestive diseases	6.5	11.8	8.1	12.6	10.2
Verminosis (worm diseases)	7.2	6.3	8.0	13.0	7.6
Gastro-enteritis	3.2	8.0	15.4	0.0	15.4
Others	0.0	5.6	15.4	24.2	16.7

Source: CEPLANUT (1988).

It is generally considered that the causes of malnutrition are eating habits, food availability (Duboz and Vaugelade, 1988), drought and famine, and public and family hygiene (Ewbank, 1988: 96–7). These are factors closely related to the socio-economic situation and to living conditions. The rise in mortality rates reflects an 'amplification' of these factors. And structural adjustment, by reducing the quality of life, as well as the capacity of health institutions to restore health, cannot be exempted.

The educational sector

The effects of structural adjustment on education can be 'read' from the stagnation in school enrolment rates and from the decline in the quality of education. Table 12.4 gives an idea of the first effect. It is clear from this table that student enrolments continued to rise from 1970 to 1988 in absolute terms. But, meanwhile, average annual growth rates plummeted, from an average of 14.6 per cent during the pre-SAP period to an unprecedented 2.3 per cent during the programme. At least in the first year after the programme ended, the rate seems to have resumed its upward trend. However, the decline in the growth rate of secondary students actually began to be observed four years before SAP. Yet the share of current expenditures during this pre-programme period was more considerable (see Table 12.1). The beginning of this trend may therefore be explained by the linkage effects of a decline in the quality of education at the primary level, something which would require further investigation.

Table 12.4 Trend of secondary school enrolments in Zaire in 1970–71 and 1987–8

School years	Total (boys and girls)	Girls	Annual growth rates
1970/1	202,033	43,335	–
1971/2	299,611	70,339	48.30
1972/3	324,966	81,950	8.46
1973/4	286,272	68,495	–11.90
1974/5	446,644	118,818	56.00
1975/6	511,481	135,341	14.51
1976/7	599,412	158,374	17.20
1977/8	704,332	186,312	17.50
1978/9	830,429	220,309	17.90
1979/80	845,577	227,693	1.82
1980/1	861,774	235,610	1.95
1981/2	879,057	244,099	2.00
1982/3	897,468	253,203	2.09
1983/4	917,052	262,966	2.18
1984/5	937,859	273,442	2.26
1985/6	959,934	284,686	2.35
1986/7	983,334	296,750	2.43
1987/8	1,066,351	342,425	8.44

Source: Ministry of Primary and Secondary Education, Educational Planning and Statistics Directorate.

Whatever the case, it is clear that structural adjustment did not succeed in correcting this trend. Since educational institutions could not expand their intake capacity (owing undoubtedly to the cut in funds allocated to education dictated by SAP), they were no longer capable of accommodating more pupils and students. Furthermore, since population growth rates continued to rise during the period, there is reason to believe that illiteracy rates also worsened in Zaire, although we have no statistics to demonstrate that. Concerning the quality of education, several factors need to be considered simultaneously, namely, the rate of increase in student enrolments, the intake capacity of educational institutions, and the budget allocated to education. We have already noted that enrolments continued to increase, while the intake capacity remained at the same (or almost the same) level and budget allocations to education dwindled considerably. The consequence was undoubtedly a decline in the quality of education, although, once again, we have no statistics reflecting this decline.

The decline in the quality of education seems to have been considerable at the higher education level, where student enrolments for the first year continued to

Table 12.5. Access of qualified students to higher education, entry to first year, 1975–89

Years	Qualified students	Number admitted	Growth rates
1975/6	18,581	9200	–
1976/7	17,064	10,396	13.0
1977/8	–	11,019	6.0
1978/9	17,733	11,680	6.0
1979/80	20,701	9695	–16.9
1980/1	24,102	11,945	23.2
1981/2	20,530	10,070	–15.7
1982/3	26,026	14,715	46.1
1983/4	34,650	12,395	–15.8
1984/5	38,157	14,689	18.5
1985/6	42,264	17,760	20.9
1986/7	40,913	21,069	18.6
1987/8	52,715	23,040	9.3
1988/9	49,840	28,819	25.1
1989/90	53,360	30,900	7.2

Source: Ministry of Higher and University Education, Academic Service Department.

increase (Table 12.5) in spite of limited places and dwindling operating costs. In fact, higher educational and university institutions took in, on average, 11,090 students each year between 1975 and 1983, as against 16,478 during the SAP period and 27,586 since 1987. Table 12.6 below shows the declining average costs of training per pupil and student. It suggests that the quality of education has certainly fallen not only at the higher and university level, but also at the primary and secondary levels.

Table 12.6. Operating costs (in constant dollars) at the primary, secondary and higher education levels in Zaire

	1975	1980
Costs per primary pupil	35	29
Costs per secondary student	194	54
Costs per higher education student	2316	2271

Source: World Bank (1988).

Regardless of the level (whether primary, secondary, or higher), the average costs per pupil/student showed a downward trend between 1975 and 1980, one that was especially drastic at the secondary level. Even though there are no data over the last decade, it is quite possible, considering the reduced budgetary allocations to this sector and the increasing numbers of pupils and students, that these costs declined further for this period.

The insufficiency and deterioration of teaching materials, coupled with the ageing of laboratories, libraries, and other facilities, have all undoubtedly been worsened by this decline in the average costs of training per student. It may also be reflected in a higher frequency of drop-outs and repetitions, assumptions that would be worth verifying in future studies.

Table 12.7. Changes in Kinshasa's employment structure, 1955–84

	1955 (1)		1967 (2)		1975 (3)		1984 (4)
	No.	%	No.	%	No.	%	%
Primary sector							
– Market gardening, agriculture, fish farming	2860	2.6	2610	1.7	4500	1.3	
– Extractive industries	495	0.4	370	0.2	500	0.1	
Total primary	3355	3.0	2980	1.9	5000	1.4	9
Secondary sector							
– Processing of agricultural products	32,155	28.8	33,700	21.3	42,750		
– Other processing industries					26,600		
– Buildings and public works	24,535	22.0	13,350	8.5	26,650		
Total secondary	56,690	50.8	47,050	29.8	95,000	27.5	29
Tertiary sector							
* Formal tertiary							
– Commerce, banking-services	15,772	14.1	30,260	19.2	20,000		
– Transport and communications	16,825	15.1	20,700	13.7	50,000	14.5	
– Administration					75,000		
– Army	9167	8.2	43,320	27.5	12,000		
– Personnel services and others	9555	8.5	10,930	6.9	13,000		
* Informal tertiary							
– Small-scale socio-economic activities	–		15,000		28,000		
– Permanent market sellers	–		–		45,000		
– Miscellaneous	–				2000		
* Miscellaneous	360	0.3	2520	1.6			
Total tertiary	51,679	46.2	107,730	68.3	245,000	71.0	63
TOTAL	111,724	100.0	157,760	100.0	345,000	100.0	

Sources: (1) According to AIMO quoted by Pain (1984: 106);
(2) According to INS quoted by Pain (1984: 106);
(3) According to BEAU quoted by Pain (1984: 106);
(4) According to 1984 Census in INS (1991).

The employment sector

Employment is one sector that was directly affected by structural adjustment measures. Many teachers and especially civil servants were retired prematurely on the recommendation of the structural adjustment programme, the idea being to reduce the government's wage bill. Since 1987, the government has retired 15,000 civil servants. Apart from this direct impact, trends in Zaire's employment structure may also be revealing. It appears that the structural adjustment measures make the creation of new jobs virtually impossible for the moment. Hence, due to population pressures on the one hand, and the large number of secondary school certificate holders and of higher education graduates in search for jobs on the other, the informal sector is proving to be the only 'sheet anchor' for job-seekers, as well as for the government, which has been expected to procure jobs for them.

In Table 12.7, we review the trends in Kinshasa's employment structure, using data collected by various bodies and agencies. Even though the years of structural adjustment are not covered, the data may nevertheless be useful for purposes of extrapolation.

Although the proportion of civil servants showed no decline, this could be explained by the fact that the retrenchment measures did not begin until the SAP period, for which we have no detailed data. However, the population employed in the informal sector increased considerably between 1967 and 1975, rising from 15,000 to 28,000. This seems to have operated to the detriment of the primary and secondary sectors. Although a decline would be 'normal' for the primary sector due to the modernization of the economy, reduction in employment levels in the secondary sector reflects a lack of economic buoyancy in enterprises.

The growth of employment in the informal sector observed up to 1975 is likely to have continued or even intensified during the SAP period, when there were not only retrenchments of civil servants, but also a deterioration in living conditions and problems in creating new jobs. On the relationship between the deterioration of living conditions and the growth of the informal sector, Pain (1984) has showed that this sector absorbs not only the unemployed, but also wage earners seeking to 'round off' their end-of-month salaries, as well as the wealthy in search of profitable opportunities.

Conclusion and Recommendations

To demonstrate the impact of the structural adjustment programmes on social sectors is no mean task. Nevertheless, we have focused attention on a certain number of variables for which data are available for Kinshasa or the entire country. The trends they reveal suggest that structural adjustment has had a clear negative impact on the social sectors. This was especially evident in that adjustment measures brought a decline in the current (and operating) expenditures of these sectors. The share of the budget devoted to running education, for example, was only 0.7 per cent during the structural adjustment period, as against 22.7 per cent for the period immediately before. For health, the percentages were 1.2 and 4 per cent, respectively.

The impact of such under-financing on these social sectors was quickly felt:

- on the health sector, where the prevalence and mortality rate of infectious and parasitic diseases continued to increase in Kinshasa. The situation was the same for nutritional diseases, which have become increasingly deadly;

- on the educational sector, where a stagnation in secondary-school enrolments was observed and the quality of education at the primary and secondary as well as the higher education level seems to have been negatively affected;

- on the employment sector, where there had been a retrenchment of civil servants as well as a 'swelling' of the informal sector.

The implementation of the structural adjustment programme in Zaire thus seems to have produced two opposite effects. There was, on one hand, an improvement in the macro-economic situation, while on the other hand, the population's living conditions greatly deteriorated. It was for this reason that the structural adjustment programme set up in 1987 could not be carried through to the end.

Structural adjustment programmes may be necessary to get Zaire's economy out of its impasse. But these programmes should certainly take into account their negative and undesirable effects on the social sectors. It was for this reason that Zaire has in addition implemented an Adjustment Programme for Social Sectors (PASS). Its objectives are:

- to halt the deterioration of social sector programmes by restoring an appropriate level of financing in the medium term;

- to improve the efficiency of these sectors, by better distributing responsibilities between the public and non-governmental sectors;

- to improve equity in access to social services, both at the geographic and economic levels, with priority being given to the protection of the most underprivileged social classes;

- to set up new inter-sectoral activities aimed at promoting the long-term development of human resources.

The evaluation of the social effects of structural adjustment and of any economic pump-priming programmes should become a routine task. This would make it possible to correct, on a continuous basis, the strategies adopted, and to avoid sacrificing the people for whom the policies were originally envisaged and designed. A Permanent Bureau for Economic Policy Evaluation should be set up to this end, run by a multi-disciplinary scientific team.

As we have seen, better understanding of the social effects of structural adjustment has been 'handicapped' by the absence of appropriate data. The World Bank has recommended the organization of large-scale data collection operations connected with these aspects and their analysis, a suggestion that has been taken up in some African countries, such as Côte d'Ivoire. It would therefore be expedient, in view of the magnitude of the impact of structural adjustment in Zaire, to undertake such surveys in this country. The data collected would make it possible to verify the assertions advanced in this study, and to work out appropriate remedies.

References and Bibliography

Banque du Zaire. *Rapports annuels.* Kinshasa.

E. Bobwa (1988). 'La morbidité des adultes par cause de décés dans trois centres hospitaliers de Kinshasa en 1981, 1984 et 1987'. Mémoire de licence en démographie, Université de Kinshasa.

CEPLANUT (1988). *Résultats de l'étude des archives de l'Hôpital pédiatrique de Kalembelembe (1982–6).* No. 52. Kinshasa.

Economic Commission for Africa (1989). *Cadre africain de référence pour les programmes d'ajustement structurel en vue du redressement et de la transformation socio-économique (CARPAS).* E/ECA/CM.15/6/Rev.3. Addis Ababa.

Département de l'Agriculture et du Développement Rural (1987). *Situation actuelle de l'agriculture zaïroise.* Projet 660-070/USAID/PRAGMA CORP.

Département du Plan (1987, 1988 et 1989). *Document-cadre de politique économique.* Kinshasa: mimeograph.

P. Duboz and J. Vaugelade (1988). 'La malnutrition comme facteur de risque de la mortalité', *UIESP–UEPA, Actes du Congrès africain de population.* Vol. 2, pp. 3.5.17.–3.5.30.

D. Ewbank (1988). 'La santé en Afrique', in *UIESP: L'état de la démographie africaine:* 87–104.

J. Gregory and V. Piche (1986). *Population, santé et développement: cadre conceptuel, variables clés et possibilités méhodologiques.* Université de Montréal, Département de Démographie, Collection de Tirés à part.

C. Grootaert and R. Kanbur (1990). *Analyse opérationnelle de la pauvreté et des dimensions sociales de l'ajustement structurel.* DSA, Document de travail No. 1. Washington, DC: World Bank.

Institut national de la statistique (INS) (1991). *Zaïre – Un aperçu démographique.* Kinshasa.

Institut de recherches économiques et sociales (IRES). *Indices des prix.*

Mosley and Chen (1985). 'An Analytical Framework for the Study of Child Survival in Developing Countries' *Population and Development Review*, No. 10: 5–24.

M. Pain (1984). *Kinshasa – La ville et la cité.* Paris: Orstom, Collection Mémoires, No. 105.

R. Pineault and C. Daveluy (1986). *La planification de la santé – concepts, méthodes, stratégies.* Montréal: Agence d'Arc Inc.

World Bank (1988). *L'éducation en Afrique subsaharienne – pour une stratégie d'ajustement, de revitalisation et d'expansion.* Washington, DC.

World Bank (1989). *World Bank Annual Report 1989.* Washington, DC.

World Bank (1990). *World Development Report: Poverty.* Washington., DC

Index